THE MINISTRY OF THE FATHER'S HEART

DIVINE RESTORATION

EMBRACING A LIFE FREE FROM FEAR

HEATHER THOMPSON

*"The Spirit of the Sovereign Lord is on me,
because the Lord has anointed me
to proclaim good news to the poor.*

*He has sent me to bind up the broken-hearted,
to proclaim freedom for the captives
and release from darkness for the prisoners,
to proclaim the year of the Lord's favour
and the day of vengeance of our God,*

*to comfort all who mourn,
and provide for those who grieve in Zion—
to bestow on them a crown of beauty
instead of ashes,
the oil of joy
instead of mourning,
and a garment of praise
instead of a spirit of despair.
They will be called oaks of righteousness,
a planting of the Lord for the display of his splendour."*

Isaiah 61:1-3

Dedication

To all on the Ministry Team who cared for
those who were traumatised and broken-hearted.
This is your story too.

DIVINE RESTORATION
Copyright © 2024 Heather Thompson

ISBN: 978-1-915223-28-9

All rights reserved.

No part of this publication may be reproduced, stored in a retrieval system, or transmitted in any form or by any means, electronic, mechanical, photocopying or otherwise, without prior written consent of the publisher except as provided by under United Kingdom copyright law. Short extracts may be used for review purposes with credits given.

Main translation in use: NIV

THE HOLY BIBLE, NEW INTERNATIONAL VERSION®, NIV® Copyright © 1973, 1978, 1984, 2011 by Biblica, Inc.® Used by permission. All rights reserved worldwide.

Scripture quotations marked TPT are from The Passion Translation®. Copyright © 2017, 2018, 2020 by Passion & Fire Ministries, Inc. Used by permission. All rights reserved. ThePassionTranslation.com.

Scripture taken from the New King James Version®. Copyright © 1982 by Thomas Nelson. Used by permission. All rights reserved.

Scripture is taken from GOD'S WORD®. © 1995, 2003, 2013, 2014, 2019, 2020 by God's Word to the Nations Mission Society. Used by permission.

Scripture quotations marked MSG are taken from THE MESSAGE, copyright © 1993, 2002, 2018 by Eugene H. Peterson. Used by permission of NavPress. All rights reserved. Represented by Tyndale House Publishers, Inc.

Scripture quotations taken from the (NASB®) New American Standard Bible®, Copyright © 1960, 1971, 1977, 1995, 2020 by The Lockman Foundation. Used by permission. All rights reserved. www.lockman.org

The Living Bible copyright © 1971 by Tyndale House Foundation. Used by permission of Tyndale House Publishers Inc., Carol Stream, Illinois 60188. All rights reserved. The Living Bible, TLB, and The Living Bible logo are registered trademarks of Tyndale House Publishers.

Scripture quotations are from The ESV® Bible (The Holy Bible, English Standard Version®), © 2001 by Crossway, a publishing ministry of Good News Publishers. Used by permission. All rights reserved.

Scripture quotations marked (NLT) are taken from the *Holy Bible*, New Living Translation, copyright ©1996, 2004, 2015 by Tyndale House Foundation. Used by permission of Tyndale House Publishers, Carol Stream, Illinois 60188. All rights reserved.

Publisher's statement: Throughout this book, the love for our God is such that whenever we refer to Him, we honour with capitals. On the other hand, when referring to the devil, we refuse to acknowledge him with any honour to the point of violating grammatical rule and withholding capitalisation.

Published by
Maurice Wylie Media
Your Inspirational & Christian Publisher

For more information visit
www.MauriceWylieMedia.com

Endorsement

There is a vital and important section in this book where Heather deals in depth with the subject of Fragmentation, explaining different ways in which a person may fragment in their soul and spirit as a consequence of trauma and how this affects them. Trauma may perhaps be the result of an accident, of sudden fear, or of physical, psychological or sexual abuse. Also included is a section on Intruder Fragmented Human Spirits, their role and function, and how they impact lives. Heather covers all these aspects of fragmentation expertly and fully. This ministry is done lovingly and gently because the fragmented person-part needs to feel loved, safe and secure as they face and walk through the trauma that has caused their separation from life.

On one occasion I was praying with a thirty-year old woman when, suddenly, she changed and became a little girl. I was taken aback but, with hindsight, it was God showing me that this person had fragmented when young and that this little girl was part of the woman at the time. Not knowing how to resolve this, I took the lady to see Heather. When the little girl, aged six, appeared once again she appeared to be deeply traumatised. Over a number of weeks Heather and I ministered to her and towards the end of ministry, Heather asked her whether she would like some sweets the next time she came to see us. Sure enough, as soon as the little girl surfaced the following week in ministry she asked for the sweets. An adult would not do that. As a result of gentle patient ministry, the little girl was healed, grown up, and restored back to where she belonged as part of the adult.

Through experiences such as this, I came to the understanding that praying for a person who has fragmented does not always bring healing unless the fragmented person-part is healed first through gentle prayer and ministry.

Rev. Jim Hagan B.D., September 2022.
Minister Emeritus, Donacloney Presbyterian Church, Lurgan, Northern Ireland.

Contents

Forewords   **11**

Introduction   **15**

Section 1: Treasure uncovered   **19**

1.1   Discovering Hidden Treasure   21
1.2   Healing Those who have been Fragmented in Soul and Spirit through Trauma   27
1.3   Fully Fragmented Person-parts and their Restoration   41
1.4   Other Forms of Fragmented Person-parts and their Restoration   71
1.5   Fragmentations which do not Belong to the Person or are False   101

Section 2: Heart Matters   **113**

2.1   Healing of the Heart   115
2.2   The Inner Child and Prodigal and their Restoration   119
2.3   The Alter Ego and Core Identity and their Restoration   143

Section 3: Trauma held in the body   **163**

3.1   Releasing Trauma from the Body   165

Section 4: Truth — **171**

4.1 Truth Uncovered — 173
4.2 Knowing God as the Healer of our Souls — 175

Section 5: Love — **183**

5.1 Journey out of Fear and into Divine Love — 185

Section 6: Our Father's Love Song Over Us — **219**

6.1 Our Father God's Love for Us — 221

Glossary — **229**

Contact — **230**

Foreword One

Have you ever had feelings of inferiority, insecurity and inadequacy? Do you ever hear choruses playing in your mind over and over again, telling you either that you are useless or a failure? You may have been walking with Jesus Christ for years and yet there is the lingering sting of old regrets; a temptation to which you all too readily succumb; a divided heart that pulls you in different directions at the same time; or an overriding cloud of fear or anxiety that never seems to go away? There is something deep down that binds you, holds you back or frustrates you.

The prophet Isaiah announced that the Lord came to set the captives free, to comfort those who mourn, "to bestow on them a crown of beauty instead of ashes, the oil of gladness instead of mourning and a garment of praise instead of a spirit of despair." On one level, you know the truth of these words, but for some reason they have not yet become a living reality for you. They seem like poetic licence, pie-in-the sky, wishful thinking, unattainable. And yet you have an abiding longing not to live your life in various shades of grey but in full colour.

If this even remotely describes you, then you have found the right book at the right time. I can guarantee you that as you spend time reading these pages and assimilating their truths, the Lord Himself will guide and bring you to a place of joy, healing, restoration, freedom and wholeness.

I have been Minister of West Church, Bangor, for almost twenty-five years and have known Heather Thompson during that time as an invaluable friend and outstanding colleague in team ministry. I appreciate her loving heart, humble and gentle spirit, wisdom and discernment, patience and understanding. Time and again she has been to me personally that word of encouragement.

To know Heather is to appreciate the closeness of her walk with her heavenly Father and the intimacy she enjoys in His presence. Isaiah 61 has been her manifesto and guiding text. You will discover that the insights in this book come from a lifetime of personal devotion and waiting upon the Lord, living in obedience to His Word and being sensitive to the leading of the Holy Spirit. It is as if Heather goes ahead, opens the door and invites us to follow into ever deeper experiences of God's grace and goodness.

I have great pleasure in writing the foreword to "Divine Restoration, Embracing a Life Free from Fear", the third book in the series. I pray as you read what follows, echoing the words of Paul to the Thessalonians, that the Lord Jesus may be glorified in you and you in Him! May you discover the person God always intended you to be and reach your full potential in Him!

Very Rev Dr Charles McMullen
Minister, West Presbyterian Church, Bangor, Northern Ireland.

Foreword Two

The human mind and soul is a complex thing.

The prophet Jeremiah famously said of the heart, 'Who can know it?' It remains elusive and mysterious on many fronts. Psychology, psychiatry and neuroscience continue to make incredible discoveries about the secrets of how our brains and minds operate. However, as a species, we are still only dipping our toe into understanding the realm of the human psyche/soul.

The Bible is not a science textbook, so we should not expect intricate details about how the mind and soul function or experience dysfunction. Nevertheless, scripture is explicit on the fallenness and brokenness of our hearts. We are sick with sin and broken by our hurts. Our traumatic experiences, fraught relationships and chaotic environments can fracture our being like a shattered mosaic.

The good news is that the gospel of Jesus Christ is intended *'to heal the broken-hearted, to proclaim liberty to the captives, and the opening of the prison to those who are bound'* (Isaiah 61:1). It is often missed that the Saviour and Healer, Jesus Christ the Son of God, came into the world to *'heal the broken-hearted and bind up their wounds'* (Psalm 147:3).

"Divine Restoration, Embracing a Life Free from Fear" is a testament to Heather Thompson's many years of unswerving commitment to aiding those in need. These pages contain great wisdom from decades of her knowledge and experience, particularly in human fragmentation and the healing of the soul. I don't know anyone more proficient in these matters than her. Most importantly, Heather illuminates a path towards healing and wholeness in these pages.

This book is not what we might call 'an easy read' because much of this material will be challengingly new to most and personally poignant to some. Much thought and reflection will be needed. I have had some experience in prayer ministry over several years now, but much of this subject matter is over my head! However, I know Heather, and I know that many people have been helped by her ministry and those who ministered alongside her over decades. It seems that the Lord has brought Heather on a remarkable journey of revelation in these areas of healing both to help others and, of course, we see from her fascinating personal testimony to help herself.

May many others find healing and freedom through this volume and all the books in this trio.

David Legge
Bible Teacher, Portadown, Northern Ireland.

Introduction

The Night Watch is a magnificent painting crafted by Rembrandt in 1642. In the twentieth Century it was knifed twice and sprayed with acid yet this masterpiece has endured thanks to the generations of painter-restorers and professional conservators who have overseen its welfare.[1] Only those who understood and knew how to restore paintings could undertake this task.

There are wounds that need a sticking plaster and wounds that need more in-depth attention.

We are damaged people, living in a broken world, who often don't know where to turn for help. To whom better than to our God, our heavenly Father who created us? He reaches out to us with his heart of love to release us from our tormenting fears and rebellious ways and guide us into His rest,

> *"Come to me, all you who are weary and burdened, and I will give you rest."* Matthew 11:28

He empowers us to step out of our prisons and into the freedom that He offers so that our lives can blossom.

Over the years, many who were traumatised, tormented by fear and broken-hearted came to us believing that God could help. It was as though God, Himself, was searching them out and sending them to us.

---

1   The Art Newspaper, Nancy Kenny, 19 February 2019

Step by step He showed us in what ways each had been affected and how to minister His healing and restoration. This book tells our story.

Each one was a prisoner held captive as a consequence of trauma: fragmented in soul and spirit and suffering from emotional overload. They were living their lives under great duress and at a fraction of their potential.

Gently and lovingly God reached into the deep recesses of their lives, bringing His light into their darkness, and releasing each from their distress. He truly did

> *"bestow on them a crown of beauty instead of ashes, the oil of joy instead of mourning, and a garment of praise instead of a spirit of despair".* Isaiah 61:3

Much of what is written in this book describes healing and restoration that is supernatural and beyond human understanding. As we sought God every step of the way He directed us with verses, words that gave insight, and pictures. We understood very little at a cerebral level but walked by faith in the insights that He gave us. As time went on, we grasped the significance of what He was teaching us to a greater degree but, really, it is only as a consequence of consistent ministry over forty years that our understanding grew. Those of you who read through this book will be met with many new concepts that you may find difficult to comprehend at first. I strongly encourage you when you first read that you not worry about detail but receive whatever God focuses you on and let Him unfold any relevance for you by His Spirit.

As I have mentioned previously, anything I write is merely me sharing my story in the belief that God wants to use it to help others and it is only as we engage personally with the Spirit of God that we enter into the understanding that we need for our own healing. Although some of what is explained in this book may be used by a person on their own praying through the effect that trauma has had on them, much of the

Introduction 17

healing described here is more easily received when a person is helped by others. Miracles occurred for which we have no rational explanation but they bore fruit that lasted and demonstrated the Father-heart of God.

I pray that as you read, our heavenly Father will speak His insights and restoration to you. He is a compassionate and merciful Father who loves you unconditionally and unreservedly.

SECTION 1

TREASURE UNCOVERED

*"I will answer them before they even call to me.
While they are still talking about their needs,
I will go ahead and answer their prayers!"*

Isaiah 65:24 NLT

Chapter 1.1
Discovering Hidden Treasure

> *"He reveals deep and secret things; He knows what is in the darkness, and light dwells with Him. 'I thank You and praise You, O God of my fathers; You have given me wisdom and might, and have now made known to me what we asked of You, For You have made known to us the king's demand.'"*
> Daniel 2:22-23 NKJV

This first part of my story began when I was invited to join two others in ministering to a young woman. What took place was totally unexpected and proved to be the beginning of a ministry that has continued for forty years. Up until that time, I had been helping people through a process called Inner Healing or Healing of Emotions (A Journey of Discovery) which sometimes necessitated Spiritual Warfare (Unveiling our True Identity in Christ). For many sufferers, this is sufficient.

Having completed several sessions with one lady (different lady),[2] we were surprised when one day she changed in front of us into a distressed four-year old. Our response was to comfort the child and encourage her to share with us what was troubling her. Little by little, as the child began to share what had happened, we realised that this traumatic event had happened when the lady was the age of this child.

---

2   c.f. Endorsement by Rev. Jim Hagan.

We talked with the child about what she was remembering. While observing her we witnessed emotional responses that were distressing her and so asked Jesus to remove them from her and give her His peace. She gradually became settled, then disappeared, and the lady came to the surface once again. We talked together about what had happened and learnt that the lady had been aware of what had just taken place but could not recall from memory the incident that the child had described.

About a month later when, in conversation with this same lady, a deeply upset five-year old child appeared. Again, we gently comforted her and listened to her story. She was afraid and so we asked Jesus to take her fear (emotional) and also deliver her from an evil spirit of fear. After this the child became content and disappeared.

With each of these children we had been using what we already knew about ministering inner healing and deliverance. It was only later that we understood the significance of the fact that two child-parts of this lady had surfaced.

When young, this lady had been so traumatised on two occasions that a part of her, with the memory of the incident and the associated emotional responses, had been separated in some way from the rest of her. As she continued to grow, these traumatised parts had remained buried within her at the ages at which the traumas had occurred and she had grown up without conscious awareness of them. We refer to them as fragmented person-parts because they are caused when a person fragments into two or more parts as a consequence of some traumatic event in their life.

We ministered to the lady, step by step asking God questions and following His leading. Frequently we were directed to scriptures. We were careful not to influence the lady or any of her child-parts. So began the development of our understanding as to what had happened in her past, what was currently happening, and how God wanted us to help this lady to become free.

This was our introduction to healing and restoring parts of a person who had fragmented early in life. Each of these fragmented child-parts was like buried treasure waiting to be found and nurtured into full potential before being intermingled back into the person to whom they belonged. The restoration of fragmented child-parts is accomplished through the love of the Father-heart of God for His children. It is a ministry that fills us with wonder and touches us with a sense of being on holy ground.

It was a couple of months later before we (myself and co-counsellor) witnessed the appearance of another child-part. This same lady had become increasingly distressed for no known reason. When we met with her to try and understand what was causing her anguish a six-year-old appeared in her place, curling herself up on the seat. We spoke gently to her, reassuring her that she was in a safe place and repeating words of comfort to her.

Earlier that day God had shown one of us a picture in which a wee girl was running freely in green fields. Since God brought this back to mind, we shared it with her believing it might help her. Gradually as we talked, the child relaxed and then began to share a picture she could see in her mind: she was playing with a grown up and she liked her. She then talked about having been in a dark place. As I listened, I recalled that God had brought Isaiah 9:2 to my mind earlier that day and that He intended me to tell her about it now as it would show her that He had known about her being in the dark,

> *"The people walking in darkness have seen a great light; on those living in the shadow of death, a light has dawned."*

I explained what the verse meant; that Jesus was the light who had come to bring her out of darkness. It seemed a good time to introduce ourselves and we then spent time getting to know one another and helping her to be able to trust us. She told us that when she cried, her mummy never came to help her and that she had never been hugged or told that she was loved. We suggested that she ask Jesus what He thought of her.

He told her that she was His precious child. We decided to call her, "Precious Child", thus reinforcing this truth.

She told us that she would like to be a big girl so we asked Jesus whether she could grow up. As we led her in a prayer to that effect, He slowly grew her to age seven, stopping occasionally where there was a distressing memory.

We asked her what it felt like to be at age seven and chatted a bit about Jesus and how He helps people. We were building her knowledge of, and confidence in, Jesus, hoping that she would choose at some stage to ask Him into her life. We let her decide what she wanted to talk about while using any opportunity to affirm her. As ministry continued, she was grown up to twelve years old and, in one of her chats with Jesus, she chose to ask Him into her life to help her.

Shortly thereafter she became extremely frightened and then began to describe what was happening. As we ministered to her, we were guided to release her from some evil spirits whereupon she once again became relaxed and peaceful, no longer afraid. We told her how the Holy Spirit helps us through talking to us and giving us insights that guide us in helping her. She responded by wanting Him to help her in that way, and so we guided her in asking Him to fill her and give her His gifts. She told us that she could see the words, "love, peace, joy". Content, we all relaxed together and chatted for a while. Ministry continued throughout the day as the child was progressively grown up to age nineteen. At this point she was very tired, so we asked Jesus to hold her in His arms so that she could sleep. She disappeared and the adult person-part came to the surface once again, and we talked through all that had taken place. What an amazing day it had been! As I reflect on it now on, I am reminded of the scripture,

> *"Teach me Your ways that I might continue to find favour in Your sight."* Exodus 33:13

All that follows in this book is a consequence of God teaching us step by step how to bring freedom to people, some of whom had fragmented as children and had buried child-parts (chapters 1.2-1.5) and others in whom the pressures of life had built up to such an extent that their hearts were fractured (chapters 2.1-2.3). This ministry continued for many years in the background of our Church life and was never advertised but, somehow, God brought many desperate people to us who had given up hope of ever being free from torment.

Early on in this ministry, we asked God to give us a scripture to describe it. He referred us to Ephesians 3:10-11,

> *"His intent was that now, through the church, the manifold wisdom of God should be made known to the rulers and authorities in the heavenly realms, according to his eternal purpose that he accomplished in Christ Jesus our Lord."*

This passage has been our great encouragement at times when it seemed that we were on a cliff edge. We learnt that God often leaves the rescue strategy until the very last second so that the enemy thinks he is winning. Then comes the showdown! What a privilege to belong to Jesus, partnering with Him as He brings in His Kingdom on earth.

Chapter 1.2
Healing Those who have been Fragmented in Soul and Spirit through Trauma

---

"For you created my inmost being; you knit me together in my mother's womb. I praise you because I am fearfully and wonderfully made; your works are wonderful; I know that full well."
Psalm 139:13-14

Jesus told His disciples that, if they held to His teaching, they would know the truth and the truth would set them free.[3] All ministry that sets the captives free rests on knowing, believing and applying the revelation that the Holy Spirit brings through the truths of scripture and in the name of Jesus.

As we journey with God our Father, we can enter into this freedom one step at a time as the Holy Spirit lights up our path. This freedom, true freedom within ourselves with others and with God, comes when we reach the place where we truly know deep within who we really are in Christ and what we really want as His children. Knowledge of this truth lies deep within each of us but may have become buried through sin and its consequences, and through hurtful relationships, circumstances or trauma. When a person is fully restored into this truth, the treasure that is within them, and which has been buried, emerges in all its beauty and

---

[3] John 8:31-32.

power. Our long-held coping and denial mechanisms are dismantled, our brokenness is healed, and our souls are set free to align with our spirits and so follow the Holy Spirit without inner struggle.

God wants to have a loving relationship with each of us, one in which we get to know Him and His ways better and through which we receive His healing and guidance. Such a close relationship requires two-way conversation that in time leads to us opening our hearts increasingly to Him and receiving more revelation about Him and His ways. It was through having this kind of two-way conversation with God that He instructed us in how we should proceed in this ministry to those who had been fragmented through trauma. As a consequence, many were healed, restored, and released into a confident knowledge and security, knowing deep within their innermost being who they truly are in Christ.

God wants us to know the specific plans and purposes He has for each of us in this life. Generally, He wants us to have relationships with others that mirror the love that He has for us, and so He calls upon us all to reach out to others, meeting their needs in Christ Jesus whether through evangelism, through feeding the hungry, through healing and releasing the afflicted in body, mind and spirit, through administration, through intercession, or through some other gifting. These relationships develop as we worship together and enjoy friendship through fellowship, relate to one another in the workplace and where we live, and care for one another, wherein we do that for which He has equipped us,

> *"For we are His workmanship, created in Christ Jesus for good works, which God prepared beforehand that we should walk in them."* Ephesians 2:10

The call upon each person is unique and can only be fulfilled in its specific nature by that person. Our unique gifting complements that of others so that, as a whole, we function as the Body of Christ here on this earth. It is important to make it clear at the outset of this section that it will be focussing in a specific way on the effects that trauma can have on a person's life. What follows does not apply to everyone but may be useful to many.

As I entered into the mysteries of releasing the captives,[4] this poem[5] resonated over and over again in my spirit,

> *And I said to the man who stood at the gate of the year:*
>
> *"Give me a light, that I may tread safely into the unknown!"*
>
> *And he replied: "Go out into the darkness and put your hand into the Hand of God. That shall be to you better than light and safer than a known way."*
>
> *So, I went forth, and finding the Hand of God, trod gladly into the night. And He led me toward the hills and the breaking of day in the lone East.*

As I put my hand in the hand of God and called out to Him from my perplexity, He answered me and told me great and hidden things that I had not known.[6] I learnt over and over again that,

> *"He reveals the deep things of darkness and brings utter darkness into the light."* Job 12:22

and,

> *"There is a God in heaven who reveals mysteries...."* Daniel 2:28

and gives us,

> *"The treasures of darkness."* Isaiah 45:3

---

4   Isaiah 61:1-3.
5   Excerpt from poem, *At the Gate of the Year*, Minnie Louise Harkins 1875-1957
6   Jeremiah 33:3.

Paul referred to this power of the Spirit that is at work in any person who relies wholly on God,

> *"And so, it was with me, brothers and sisters. When I came to you, I did not come with eloquence or human wisdom as I proclaimed to you the testimony about God. For I resolved to know nothing while I was with you except Jesus Christ and him crucified. My message and my preaching were not with wise and persuasive words, but with a demonstration of the Spirit's power, so that your faith might not rest on human wisdom, but on God's power."* 1 Corinthians 2:1-2, 4-5.

My understanding of fragmentation is as follows.

God creates each of us in His own image,

> *"So, God created mankind in his own image, in the image of God he created them; male and female he created them."* Genesis 1:27

Each of us was created as one spirit, having one soul and living in one body. When a person becomes fragmented that one spirit and/or one soul may become broken, fragmenting into one or more parts but remaining attached to, and living in, the one body and connected to that part of the spirit and soul that remains functioning in the body.

There are expressions of this in folklore and history and, indeed, in many of our modern films and dramas. Fragmentation of a person can be likened to the scattering that can occur between members of a family when their relationships break down. Even when apart, no-one ceases to belong to the family, and the hurt or pain that any one member is going through has a painful effect on the rest of the family until it is resolved. Where there is unconditional love and acceptance, family members will return one by one until all are reunited as a family again. In scripture we read that where there was persecution of the Church there was scattering also,

> *"On that day a great persecution broke out against the church in Jerusalem, and all except the apostles were scattered throughout Judea and Samaria."* Acts 8:1

This scattering led to the believers growing in boldness and to the church growing, and even though physically separated they remained spiritually bound together as one in the Body of Christ.

The experience and subsequent healing of all those who have become fragmented is similar but uniquely applied. The unconditional love and acceptance of God the Father touching the person leads to trust in Him and willingness to receive insight and to respond. Complete restoration takes place when all divisions are removed and person-parts are intermingled together. The person is thus completely released from the captivity that has occurred and is restored to being one spirit with one soul as God created. In a way it is similar to the strengthening that develops within church fellowships when differences are worked through with mutual respect, and unity is restored.

Each fragmented part uses all the physiological functions of the body and so, if they surface, can appear as a complete person. Each fragmentation has different characteristics and behaves according to age and experience of life. Where there is more than one fragmentation in a person each is easily recognisable by their character, language, behaviour, appearance etc. Where a person's fragmented spirit can leave the body (astral projection) there must always be at least part of the person's human spirit left actively present in the body for it to remain alive.

Although it is not normally God's preferred way, He allows a person to fragment so that those who are badly damaged and would otherwise find life unbearable, perhaps to the point of losing hope and giving up, are enabled to continue living with less turmoil than they would otherwise have.

Exceptionally, God Himself may step in and fragment a person prior to some horrific abuse which is going to be repeated over and over again at intervals. Although the same fragmented person-part, through surfacing for the repeated abuse, becomes more and more deeply traumatised, God uses this approach to protect the person as a whole from repeatedly fragmenting with each recurrence of the abuse and becoming less and less able to function in the world. In this way He protects our soul. There are many scriptures that demonstrate to us and teach us that God goes ahead of us preparing the path that we are on. Sometimes that path is fraught with evil and although God cannot stop offenders from doing what they choose to do because they have been given freedom of will, He does step in to lessen the effect or strengthen us in some way to walk through it.[7] God calls this type of fragmentation (part of the soul and part of the spirit) a personal fragmentation (chapter 1.4). His explanation for this name is that this kind of fragmentation is personal to the person.

As we study scripture, we will come to the conclusion that after the new birth our spirits cannot fragment because the Holy Spirit lives within them and has made them new.[8] Paul writes,

> *"Therefore, if anyone is in Christ, the new creation has come: The old has gone, the new is here!"* 2 Corinthians 5:17

This refers to our spirit which has been born again. The old nature of sin is blown away from our spirit (Unveiling our True Identity in Christ, section 1).

In his letter to the Ephesians Paul writes,

> *"In Him you also trusted, after you heard the word of truth, the gospel of your salvation; in whom also, having believed, you were sealed with the Holy Spirit of promise,"* Ephesians 1:13

---

7   Psalm 31:4 ESV; 41:2 ESV; 121:7 NASB
8   John 3: 3-8

Our spirits, as born-again believers, are sealed with the Holy Spirit. This means that nothing can separate our spirit from the Holy Spirit and it cannot be fragmented by trauma. Hence, once a person becomes a Christian, they will not fragment. Any earlier fragmentation however may still need restoration.

Our souls (thinking, emotions, attitudes, wills) still have to undergo transformation into alignment with Jesus.[9] Since our souls and bodies may continue to sin or be sinned against, we may need to resolve any horrific consequences of trauma. As Christians, our ability to cope with stresses and issues comes from abiding in Christ and He in us, and from receiving His grace and strength. God intends us to look to Him for help, resolving each issue as it occurs, but if, instead, we bury hurt and trauma so deeply that we delude ourselves into thinking it never took place, then what may appear to be a fragmentation but is not can occur. It is possible that we have created an alter ego (Healing of the Heart, section 2) or simply need to talk to God about the issues and resolve it with His help (Inner Healing, A Journey of Discovery, chapter 2.4).

An exception may occur when a Christian deliberately rebels against God, in which case they may then self-fragment and, consequently, part of them may become captive because of their rebellion. As long as a person chooses to reject their healed fragmented part, they will continue to have this part of them fragmented. This is all discussed later in chapter 1.4.

A person may become fragmented in soul and spirit or in soul only according to their choices and circumstances. The primary reason for the fragmenting of a person in their soul and spirit is trauma of some kind. There are many reasons and, correspondingly, there are many different ways in which people cope with their particular traumas. The presence of extreme emotional upheaval does not always imply that a person has become fragmented but may be a signal that they need some

---

9   Romans 12:2; 2 Corinthians 10:5

inner healing. Some of the causes of fragmentation in a person who has yet to come to faith in Christ are,

- abuse, whether sexual (especially rape or incest), physical, emotional or verbal
- evil or cruelty
- wickedness
- chronic or acute illness
- mental health problems
- accidents
- divorce
- severe rejection or self-rejection
- violence or mugging
- extreme fear
- birth difficulties
- operations, especially head/brain surgery
- Electroconvulsive Therapy
- emotional or spiritual deprivation
- death
- shock or trauma
- satanic/witchcraft rituals
- experiences of horror, death, war, hospitals, torture etc.
- extreme people-pleasing
- generational rights
- rebellion

- self-coping mechanism
- double-mindedness

There are three ways by which a person may fragment,

- the person themselves may (consciously or unconsciously) opt to fragment in order to cope with life
- satan or a satanist may fragment a person for evil purposes
- God may fragment a person to enable that person to cope with life despite repeated trauma[10]

Observable Symptoms and Assessment Clues to Fragmentation[11]

- irrational fears
- depression
- anxiety and panic attacks
- relationship problems
- nightmares or sleeplessness
- immaturity
- suicidal tendencies
- physical, emotional or mental illness
- a long history of help, without reaching closure
- a sense of being unable to break through
- a sense of not being present or able to be alert
- addiction

---

10 Pages 32
11 Some of these were listed in the course, "Healing the Broken Hearted", Ellel Ministries

- a symptom or difficulty that is not being healed or removed by the expected means

- unexplainable pain or torment of mind e.g., restlessness, fear, anxiety etc.

- thoughts or actions that are not in line with the person's own beliefs etc.

- unrealistic coping with issues of great magnitude

- apparent switching between two types of behaviour

In addition to those above the following may be described by the person or observed by others,

- time loss, especially if accompanied by distress (full fragmentation)

- complete change of personality or character at some point in a person's life

- out-of-character behaviour

- voice change

- change in tastes, e.g., music, TV programmes

- wearing clothing aimed at hiding self/making a statement

- some character dimension missing

- aware of absence of emotions

- excessive comforting in adults e.g., thumb sucking, comfort cloth, rocking, soft toys

- overeating/eating too little

- memory loss

- sense of feeling blocked-off in some way

- sleepwalking with a purposeful activity

- severe mood swings
- severe sexual dysfunction in marriage
- excessive identification with a group type e.g., children/teenagers, political/religious
- overwhelming tiredness accompanied by inappropriate sleeping
- apparent day dreaming, staring, trance, eye-flicking
- extreme supernatural or psychic ability
- an ability to project out of body-few fragmented parts do

Sometimes a person showing one or more of these symptoms may be emotionally broken but not fragmented. People who have fragmented are generally emotionally strong survivors.

There may be more than one fragmentation in a person and those who have been fragmented may do so in one or more ways. In some people there may be a part of the person which is normally hidden, perhaps deeply buried, but which will surface when the conditions are right. Even when buried, the thinking and emotions from any fragmented child-part can affect the person in their everyday living. Such a person suffers greatly because they cannot understand why they feel as they do and nothing that they do to try and change how they feel works for them. Relief only comes when the buried part is healed and restored to their rightful place whether it surfaces or not.

In some, the fragmented part may be near the surface and switch back and forth with the other part, thus causing confusion. For example, one person who was struggling with his memory came for prayer. God revealed that he had become fragmented as the result of a fall as a baby. This fragmented part had periodically surfaced and then disappeared. Consequently, it appeared that this gentleman had a poor memory, recalling some things and not others. Once the two parts were intermingled and became one whole, his memory was fully restored.

Sometimes a fragmented part may surface in rebellion, do its vindictive work and then disappear again. We witnessed this in a young girl who was frequently in trouble at home but who maintained that she was not guilty of the accusations. In chapter 1.4 I will discuss some of what God taught us about different ways in which people fragment.

It is God's desire to heal us all so that we can live at our full potential. A fragmented person with one fragmentation is living at half their potential. A person with two parts fragmented may be living at less than that. A God-given gift may be locked away within a part, only becoming evident when that part is restored. When God fully heals a person, they are no longer driven by deeply held thought patterns and negative emotions.

The process of healing a person who has been fragmented is not the same as using the process of regression which encourages a person to go back in their mind to remember and face what they recall. God takes the person forward out of their pain and into a future of hope. Any trauma that surfaces from within a fragmented part of the person is in the present as far as they are concerned, and so God starts there. Step-by-step He delivers them from all their hurts and fears while growing them up through the missed years until they reach the same age as the rest of the person and are fully intermingled back into where they belong.

In ministry we must follow the leading of the Holy Spirit while He brings a fragmented part near or right up to the surface. In the previous chapter I described how we initially helped some fragmented child-parts who surfaced, and I will expand on this in the next chapter. When a person-part is near the surface the person is aware of what is disturbing them and can respond to the help the Holy Spirit offers.

Drawing, writing, playing with dolls and animals, excursions, videos – all contribute to understanding and healing. It is so beautiful to watch God relate to His children in ways that we would never dream of. At times when our explanations fail to bring reassurance, Jesus can reveal Himself and say something deeply relevant and reassuring to the child within. As they visibly relax and tell us what Jesus told them we frequently catch our breath at the wisdom of our God. We have found that many DVDs illustrate a truth that the child-part needs to embrace. Examples of some songs illustrating truth are in Aladdin ("Remain true to yourself because that is a good thing to be"), Frozen 1 ("Let it go") and Frozen 2 ("Do the next right thing"). Videos such as Ghost bring home a truth within the telling of the story (a person can still hold love in their hearts after someone they know has gone). Bible stories, nursery rhymes, secular songs, and spiritual songs are all examples of sources that God uses.

There are many ways in which a person can fragment and various reasons for the different types of fragmentation. We will consider each form in turn, and how the person is healed,

- full fragmentation
- partial fragmentation
- self-fragmentation
- slumbering spirit
- semi fragmentation
- divided soul
- torn soul
- captive spirit
- intruder spirit
- personal fragmentation
- video

Useful resources giving insight into fragmentation are the video, Frozen Peas, and the film, The Three Faces of Eve (1957), based on Corbett H

Thigpen's novel of the same name and available on YouTube and from sources such as Amazon and eBay.

It is never God's purpose that we be controlled by a person nor by a demonic spirit. The evil one seeks to bring chaos into life and does so by exerting hidden control, perhaps through trauma or satanic ritual. As an aspect of his wicked purposes, he may control a fragmented part (part of the soul and part of the spirit) into astral travel in which the person-part goes out to cause distress while at the time the body appears to be unconscious. Soul travel is different and occurs when a soul leaves a body. This is taught in some Eastern religions and practices.

Ministry to a fragmented person aims to bring wholeness and healing to the person, restoring them to what God originally intended for them. This includes removing all that is false, all that doesn't belong to the person, and ministering healing to any person-parts that have been traumatized before intermingling them back into the person, all in Jesus' name.

Chapter 1.3
Fully Fragmented Person-parts and their Restoration

"The Spirit of the Sovereign Lord is on me, because the Lord has anointed me to proclaim good news to the poor. He has sent me to bind up the broken-hearted, to proclaim freedom for the captives and release from darkness for the prisoners."
Isaiah 61:1

As I come to this part in my reflections on ministry, some scriptures revealing the heart of God become particularly relevant,

"I have come that they may have life and have it abundantly." John 10:10

"I am the way, the truth, the life." John 14:6

"Now this is eternal life: that they may know You the only true God, and Jesus Christ whom You sent." John 17:3

Many of God's people are not experiencing the abundant life that Jesus talks about. Some who are troubled have sought help from many sources and are almost afraid to hope that they can ever find a way out from their own form of captivity. Only the truth, grace and love of God can help them on their way to freedom from their turmoil, and only He can give the necessary grace and insight to those seeking to help. Paul, in his letter to the Ephesian Church, prays that, *"I keep asking that the God of our Lord Jesus Christ, the glorious Father, may give you the Spirit of wisdom and revelation, so that you may know him better. I pray that the eyes of your heart may be enlightened in order that you may know the hope to which he has called you, the riches of his glorious inheritance in his holy people"*.[12] When we listen with our spirits as well as using our natural senses, we are given insights that unfold mysteries.

Some people who suffer unbearable trauma and/or abuse become fragmented in their personhood in such a way that their fear-provoking memories and associated emotional turmoil are "forgotten". This is because a part of them, holding the pain and its cause, becomes compartmentalised and buried in some way, thus enabling the remaining part of the person to continue in relative freedom. However, since this traumatised part is still present in the person however deeply it is buried, it continues to influence the person in their decisions and emotions. The person continues through life as best they can even though functioning at less than their potential and often with an underlying sense of distress or fear.

When God brings any such person-part near or up to the surface for healing, painful issues and fear-provoking memories accompanied by emotional distress surface. Little by little we encourage the child to share what has happened. We respond with compassionate understanding while listening to God for His wisdom as to how to alleviate the distress and release the child from pain. This is the same process as inner healing (A Journey of Discovery, chapter 2.4). Deliverance from evil spirits is an integral part of this.

Once a child-part has been fully released and healed, we ask God whether they are ready to grow older. If so then we chat with the child to ensure that they are willing. As they grow through the years, they may or may not be aware of different ages that they are passing through.

---

12 Ephesians 1:17-18

Sometimes the next age they reach is that of the adult-part and it is time for each to adjust to the idea before being intermingled and healing completed. If they stop growing at an intermediate age it can be for one of two reasons. There may be another fragmented child-part of that age who has been released and healed in which case each is then prepared for intermingling together. Alternatively, this may be an age at which the child-part needs to face another fear-provoking event so as to be released and healed before growing further. Restoration is carefully orchestrated in an orderly fashion by our heavenly Father.

As we have indicated, there are different ways in which a fragmentation can occur and a person may have more than one, whether of similar type or different. In this chapter we will focus on what happens to a person when a part of them is fully fragmented.

A full fragmentation in a person is a fragmented person-part, having part of the soul and part of the spirit of the person, which becomes deeply imprisoned within the person in such a way that they have no knowledge of what is going on in the world around, remaining at the same age as the years go by. If the trauma has been one of abuse which was then repeated, whether through ritual satanic abuse or repeated molestation by the same person, the child-part surfaces at the same age as when first abused.

Distressing memories, thoughts and emotions buried within the fully fragmented part, although in the unconscious mind, filter through to the part of the person living in the present, causing underlying and inexplicable torment. Sometimes in life, some trigger may cause a fragmented part to appear, leading to great distress and confusion for the person and those near to them.

This full fragmentation of a person can be described as that part being so frightened that they run away as far as they can from the terror, eventually entering a "room" and closing the door. Once in the closed room they can't and don't want to open it because they are so frightened, and therefore they remain in the dark. To all appearances it is as though that part is asleep. Thus, the conscious knowledge of the abuse becomes lost to the rest of the person.

It may appear as though only the memories of experiences, and the associated thought patterns and feelings are locked away in the unconscious mind. However, along with these, a part of the person's spirit is also deeply buried because they have been abused in a way that has affected them spiritually. Even when a child is young and doesn't understand that what is happening through abuse is wrong, they may sense violation in their spirits. If a child truly believes that the abusing person really loves them, they may not fragment but this is unusual. The outcome of any trauma depends on what is happening in the child's spirit and soul. Often an abuser will indoctrinate the child into believing that they are bad and that the abuser has their good in mind. They may be told that the abuse is to make them good. The child may think of it as "sore love". The consequences are serious as the person growing up believes inherently that they are bad and doesn't deserve anything good to happen for them, and finds it difficult to believe that God loves them and wants them to have good in their life.

As long as a child is under the jurisdiction of parents or guardians who are evil in intent, the abuse may continue until the child grows up and breaks away. God will not prevent this because He has given everyone free will; nevertheless, He is present with both the child to comfort and with the abuser to convict. Once the child becomes an adult and is free to make their own choices, then God when asked is able to move in that person's life and, with their cooperation, free them.

All healing demonstrates God's great compassion and mercy. There is no pattern to it as God loves each of us as individuals and treats us as such. He alone knows and understands the best way in which to release us.

Where a person has chosen to love God with heart and mind and soul, and to resist fleshly desires within, God may sovereignly choose to honour that choice by freeing them from the effects of abuse without their conscious awareness. This may include healing fragmented parts back into the adult without them consciously knowing.

But His mercy is also seen in the process of healing a person by walking with them step by step through to complete restoration, using the intervening time to disciple and strengthen them, and give them insight and understanding so that in turn they can help others. It is this latter approach to healing that we describe in this book.

Ministry

When a person comes for ministry because they are distressed, they may not know the reason but, as they settle in a safe environment sharing in what ways they are troubled, the Holy Spirit will guide each person present towards understanding.

If the person has been fragmented as a child, then gradually the memories and accompanying emotions within the traumatised child-part will begin to move from the unconscious to the subconscious mind sometimes in the form of flashbacks or in new dreams which may be repetitive. This is an important stage in ministry and the person needs affirmation and support in what they are experiencing.

What has become evident is that this ministry to people, who have been fragmented in some way, begins when they recognise for themselves that their issues and struggles don't seem to come directly from any consciously held memories, emotions or thinking, or as a consequence of their present life situations. Sensitive exploration opens the way for trust to be built up; this is essential if a person is going to be able to share something that seems to them beyond what is normal. Little by little, as they discover that they and their story are totally acceptable and not creating waves of alarm, they begin to express more fully what seems to be happening within. They may talk about experiences such as "feeling like two different people" or "sensing or hearing a voice within". Our reassurance can settle them and lessen their fear that they're "losing it". This is the time when we can slowly strengthen them in believing that they aren't imagining things, and at the same time encourage them to use their insights to guide them forward into an understanding of what may have happened. It is vital to follow their lead and that of the Holy Spirit as they are vulnerable to being easily controlled.

Further exploration, through everyone asking God questions together, may begin to familiarise the person with some of what has happened earlier in life and which will be revealed in detail at a later date when their child-part comes to the surface. Sometimes, just before a person-part surfaces, the adult may become aware that they are responding to something in a childlike way, for example, fussing over animals and pets in an uncharacteristic way, or maybe struggling with strong unfamiliar emotions for no apparent reason.

A child-part may surface unexpectedly or the Holy Spirit may guide us to explore with the person the possibility of a fragmented child-part. Caution is needed in the latter approach, usually drawing upon carefully crafted questions based on the person's own words while watching for any physical reaction. Once the person clearly recognises that fragmentation may have occurred, we invite them to join with us in asking God to confirm this or otherwise.

Only once everyone present is confident of the direction we should take will we embark on such ministry. Ministry to a fully fragmented child-part only takes place where the adult is in agreement and willing to allow the child-part to surface. At all times they will be able to hear and feel what is happening in the interaction between the child-part and those ministering. This can be a bit scary at first for the person, so we take it extremely slowly, never pushing the person into a decision and, often, we will leave the person to think and pray about it before the next time we meet. Only when the person chooses to do so will we begin.

God brings child-parts to the surface for love and care and to experience the good things in life, each of which is an important aspect of healing and restoration. For such ministry to proceed unhindered the adult-part on the surface must be stable in their commitment to Christ, emotionally strong, and willing to trust God by yielding control to Him. Their desire to be free and whole encourages them to persevere throughout the ministry and to trust God during their strange and wonderful journey. They will have the joy of witnessing first-hand the omniscient, omnipresent and omnipotent God Almighty at work in their lives as a loving Father. Faith will increase and awareness that they are deeply loved by God will grow.

Those exercising this ministry have a great responsibility to demonstrate the unconditional love of God through being trustworthy, consistent, accepting, patient, never rushing, never controlling or manipulating. Alongside that, we facilitate inner healing within the child-part, as well as the ministry of angels, and the authority we have in Jesus' name over the demonic is key.

Before any ministry session commences, we usually in Jesus' name bind divination, deception, illusion and delusion and command them not to interfere or communicate. In doing this we are eliminating interference that could deceive. This is especially critical when we are aware that a child-part is surfacing, otherwise we could be seriously misled. Always, we have our spiritual antennae on the alert as satan has many ways in which he tries to mislead us and hinder healing. We also bind death and hell and destruction and command them to retreat in Jesus' name, and ask God to surround the child-part in peace while bringing them up. We also ask Him to surround the adult-part with His peace as He enables them to take a back seat and observe what is happening.

While we wait, we watch for clues, heed impressions coming from the Holy Spirit and listen for His instruction. He gives the necessary insight step by step as we journey with the person. When the child first surfaces, we respond to what we are sensing. The child may be distressed or fearful in which case we quietly speak peace. Sometimes gentle praying in tongues helps them as God uses this also to bring peace and assurance to them. On occasion the child-part has responded in tongues and together we have had a conversation none of which we understood. Interpretation wasn't necessary as the dialogue led to the necessary reassurance and peace. It may take a while for the child to trust as, when the child first appears, they may be terrified, blind, deaf, sleeping etc., as a consequence of what has happened to them. At this stage, as the Holy Spirit leads very gently, the child will settle down and feel comfortable and safe. During the first meeting there will often not be many words said but more an emphasis on ensuring the child-part is helped to feel safe. This may mean not touching the child, or it may mean holding their hand. Sometimes a gentle stroke on the cheek reassures. Such a child is very sensitive to touch and knows immediately from the touch whether it is "soft" or "hard", good or bad. This demonstrates to the child whether what they are being shown is "good love" or not. At some stage we introduce ourselves and tell them that Jesus loves them and has asked us to help them.

It often helps the child to have a soft toy or a doll to which they can respond. When the child has been particularly badly abused, to the point where they can't talk about themselves, or feels so insignificant that in their own minds they "don't exist" and haven't a name, they may use a soft toy or doll to voice what happened to them. In this way a child will tell you a lot about themselves, how they are feeling and what has been happening in their lives through the "words" of the toy. They will also talk to the toy as if it were a person and provide the answers from the toy. Sometimes Jesus will use such an opportunity to provide the answer that He wants the child to hear.

As each child-part grows in trust of Jesus through experiencing, talking and listening to Him, we can learn so much about how Jesus loves everyone and how He ministers in unique ways to each part. He truly is unconditional love, never condemning, never focussing on what the person feels guilty about, but rather always providing a way forward in security and peace.

Usually, the child-part will eventually become tired and so we will suggest they go with Jesus for a sleep. When the adult-part surfaces again, we spend time with them ensuring that they know and understand all that has taken place. Often, they give us helpful insights as to how the child-part was feeling or what they were thinking, and this knowledge can contribute to the next session.

Much of what we have to talk about in terms of memories is very difficult because of its brutality for both the child and for those ministering healing, but God has a way of making even hard things bearable for us all. Often, He will encourage a fun time prior to a difficult session of ministry where horrendous memories need to be faced. At times His sense of humour comes through in the things He says to the child and to us. Always, we are being touched very deeply by the compassion, love and wonder of God. This is truly a miraculous healing ministry, very gentle and fruitful.

We take things slowly in order to find out what we can without frightening the child. Each child has different fears and has been affected in different ways by these fears. One child-part had decided not to see what was happening to her; she had caused herself to be "blind" and was therefore unable to see as she surfaced. Gentle exploration with the help of the Holy Spirit led to our being able to resolve this with her. As we talk gently and sensitively, we are building up trust. We are careful to follow the promptings of the Holy Spirit as to when the child needs a rest, a diversion, or some fun.

The child-part may not have any experience of relationships that are wholesome nor of being held with unconditional love that is pure and will not betray or hurt. They may not have experience of play or of the outside world. They are frequently malnourished mentally, spiritually and physically. A disorder, such as an eating disorder, in the adult-part of a person may originate in a child-part. If so, this needs to be resolved in the child-part before intermingling them together as generally speaking, it is easier to resolve problems with the child-part rather than after joining has taken place. If there has been physical injury at the time of the accident or incident, it may be locked into a fragmented part and healing may not come for the adult-part until that child-part is released from the causal effects. If a person has been fragmented because of shock e.g., a car accident, then the shock must be lifted off the fragmented part in Jesus' name and the part reassured and allowed to talk through the event and receive emotional release from their distress and anguish.

Frequently, the person has believed lies about themselves as a consequence of what they have experienced and, although what has happened is fact and cannot be changed, the way the person thinks and feels about it may be a misconception leading to self-rejection. Through love, God helps the child-part to have a different perspective on the people or events which have troubled them, and so they are enabled to re-interpret how they feel about themselves and others. Where the negative emotions, such as fear and self-rejection, have been intensified by evil spirits, deliverance from them frees the person to enable change in their pattern of thinking.[13]

There will be times when we just have fun, an essential aspect of restoration because these child-parts have missed out on some of the good things in life. Through various experiences and activities such as board games, physical games like hide and seek, books, videos, shopping and excursions, we arrange that the child will experience life in a new way. There are often valuable lessons in videos and stories that the child will hone in on quite naturally. As we participate in such activities, we learn about the child's feelings and mindsets. We nurture them in their knowledge of Jesus by telling them about Him and demonstrating that we talk to Him, asking for His help, often through questioning. We then encourage the child to do the same. As we listen to the answers and insights that He offers to the child we are filled with awe at how simply and easily He meets their needs. One of the wonderful truths that emerges from ministering to child-parts is the clarity and ease with which they hear Jesus (another reason to eliminate the voice of the enemy at the onset of ministry). They have no distractions, world views

---

13 2 Corinthians 10:4-5.

etc. which hinder such communication. This is a lesson we all need to learn! Frequently, through conversation with the child, the right timing presents itself in which to encourage the child-part to talk to Jesus about what He would like to happen and, eventually, the conversation leads to their asking Jesus to be their friend, to come and help them, to live within them. Jesus uses such opportunities in as many different ways as there are children. We may sense at times that Jesus wants to baptize the child in the Holy Spirit.

As we spend time with the child, we aim to replace what was stolen, or what was never there in the first place, in terms of freedom and love. In Jesus' Name, we offer security, unconditional love and acceptance, and watch in wonder as Jesus orchestrates a miracle of healing, filling in the lack in the child's life, preparing them for intermingling with the adult-part and taking their place in the outside world.

Throughout the time of restoration there is healing of memories through talking about what has happened and encouraging forgiveness and repentance wherever needed. We have to be careful in our explanations and use of language so that the child understands and is able to respond.

Frequently, there is the need to sever them from ungodly soul and spirit ties along with deliverance from evil spirits leading to subsequent infilling with the Holy Spirit (Unveiling our True Identity in Christ, section 2). Although progress can seem fairly slow in one sense, it is amazing to think that a child-part can be healed and given enough love and care and experience of life in just a few weeks to make up for a lifetime's neglect. In that time while God grows the fragmented child-part from year to year, they may experience further memories and painful emotions which we will then explore with them until they are once again at peace.

Generally, we cannot deliver child-parts from demonic spirits when they are deeply buried, but we can pray that God's love, light, etc. will penetrate, and once God brings the child-part up from the depths, more can be accomplished. Since God will do a lot of healing in the buried part while they are just below the surface, we encourage the adult person-part to participate in helping their child-part through their own love and reassurance, all the while encouraging the child into truth about Jesus.

Where there is one or more child-parts in a person, there might occur a transfer of painful emotions from the one to the other. We can pray in some way, such as asking for the cross of Jesus to be placed between child-parts and/or between any child-part and their adult-part so as to stop painful emotions being transferred from one to the other.

We need to be aware that different influences can affect the child-part. We need discernment at all times to know whether the child is acting from her own will or being controlled by an evil spirit. For example, one child-part took sweeties without asking, and we learnt from her that she had been told to. We discovered that she had a spirit of Jezebel within who had spoken to her and had offered "to help her". The child had agreed to Jezebel being in charge and so had obeyed and got into trouble. Once she understood that Jezebel was no friend she knew not to obey and we helped her to reject the spirit from being in charge. We are always encouraging any child-parts to talk to Jesus and get to know Him, and to seek His answers for themselves. This way the child-part is being prepared as a follower of Jesus before being intermingled with the adult-part.

In the stories that follow all the names given to the child-parts were given to them by Jesus as a means of identification until such time as they were healed, grown up, and intermingled with another child-part or the adult-part. These names do not reflect the actual names of the people to whom the child-parts belong. Many who came for ministry were female and this is reflected in the stories; however, this ministry is for anyone who needs it. Terms which are new will be explained in the next chapter.

Watch out for Deception!

We must remain vigilant as satan has all sorts of tricks to hinder or prevent a person from becoming free. He attempts to deceive both the child-part and those ministering healing. As we become familiar with the mannerisms and personalities of a child-part, we are less likely to be deceived, and when we depend on God to give us discernment every step of the way we need not fear being led down a wrong path as He will always bring such things into the light.

Some examples are:

- A child-part called Miriam, who was extremely sensitive to the possibility of being corrected, told me that she had heard God tell her to give me the message, "Tell Miriam to stop fidgeting". I knew that God wouldn't send me such a message and, anyway, I knew from previous sessions with Miriam that God joked with Miriam about her "wriggling". Miriam was a wriggler!

- Sometimes an evil spirit like Ahab within a child-part can confuse that part into thinking that they are someone else. Within one person there were two child-parts, Rebecca and Deborah (not their real names). Ahab confused Rebecca by telling her that she was Deborah.

- A child-part may have a demonic copy (copycat) of themselves surrounding them. It is used by the enemy to confuse ministry and aims to bring ministry to a stop because of fear of deception. In her past, a spirit of death had "befriended" Miriam through offering her an escape route whenever she wanted. Once we discovered this, we discussed with her the possibility of rejecting it, something which she found difficult to do. This was because a troublesome copycat which had been upsetting Miriam was hindering her from choosing to reject this spirit of death. After we discussed what was happening, she decided to ignore the copycat and agree to the spirit of death leaving.

Physical Illness

When sickness observed in an adult-part has its roots within a child-part, healing may need to take place in the child-part before being intermingled with the adult-part. One person who came for ministry was deteriorating in health to such an extent that she was finding it difficult to ride her horse. She was devastated because she had been told that she would eventually need a wheel chair. During ministry a fragmented child-part was healed and, consequently, the lady was physically healed.

When a physical infirmity is not due to physical causes the root cause may be resolved through one or more of the processes of inner healing, deliverance, healing and restoration of child-parts, healing of the heart and of the spirit. In the second stage, healing is completed, sometimes sovereignly, without our participation and sometimes through prayer and anointing with oil and laying on of hands.

Some adults find it difficult to receive healing even after the root causes have been removed. An example of this was a person whose root causes for Multiple Sclerosis (M.S.) were in a child-part. In ministry to this child-part, we removed lethargy of the body, soul and spirit and encouraged them to eat. We removed the "bodyguard" which the enemy had been able to put there, a spirit of fatigue, a spirit of M.S., and spirits of witchcraft and Ahab. Over time this child-part learnt to walk again and was free from the symptoms of M.S. However, when the child-part was intermingled back into the adult-part, the person still showed symptoms of M.S. and was unable to walk. We were disappointed but continue to believe and pray for her healing. Generally, child-parts receive healing easily once the root cause has been removed. However, this is not always so for the adult-part as a previously held mindset can hinder the process. One adult was afraid of losing benefits if healed and so, even though the child-part was clearly physically healed before being intermingled, the adult remained incapacitated afterwards.

I believe that there are many who have passed through the first stage of their healing and are now in a place where God will sovereignly heal them in His time.

Examples of Fragmented Child-parts in Various People who came for Ministry *(names are changed)*

Sal's story

This ministry was unusual in that it began with the child-part in the womb. When we first saw the baby, she remained still, seemed very peaceful and showed no signs of stress. While Jesus was growing her up to three months (pre-birth) she appeared to become frightened and so we prayed that the fear be taken away and that she be reassured and filled with peace. By six months her legs were moving and we observed that the fingers in her right hand were clawing at her cheek. Her body was moving slightly. Any touch from us made her jump. Again, we prayed for peace. By nine months the movements of her arms were stronger and more sweeping. Her head was moving from side to side. Her right hand was hitting out and she seemed distressed. We prayed for love and peace to surround her and that Jesus would take away her distress. She became quiet once again. Once born, Jesus grew her up little by little, first of all to three months, by which time she was moving her head. By six months she was using her hands to clutch at me with her right hand.

By age seven she was able to talk fluently and seemed to be aware that her mother had tried to abort her and her twin. At the time of the attempted abortion both she and her twin had suffered badly and her twin had died. She had felt "lonely" and "sick". We asked Jesus to heal her in her mind, emotions, spirit and body and to fill her with His Spirit. After further healing and comfort Jesus grew her up and intermingled her with her adult-part.

Matilda's Story

Matilda surfaced as a troubled five-year-old. Even though I assured her that she was important and wanted and special, she found it difficult to believe and so I suggested to her adult-part that she write notes to her child-part, affirming her in whatever way she sensed would help. I met up with the little one as often as I could and helped her through her difficult memories but, because of the need for confidentiality, I was restricted as to how much I could do with her that was fun and which would give her a taste of life beyond four walls. The adult-part contributed greatly to her well-being through buying her little craft kits, and by leaving out Disney videos and paper with colouring pencils. It became clear that she loved to draw and colour in pictures and that she enjoyed the films, each of which gave her a clear insightful message that helped her to change her thinking about herself. She told me that she was often scared and didn't think that her mummy knew, but Jesus had shown her that one day, when she was sitting on the stair feeling scared, He was sitting beside her. She struggled with tiredness all the time.

Little by little Jesus grew her up to age ten by which time I had been able to teach her how to text and phone me on the adult's phone. She had become addicted to watching the Disney film, Frozen 1, and loved to talk about it and act out the story with dolls. We talked about the need to have castles for the story and I suggested she make them out of cardboard boxes. Her adult-part left these out for her along with all sorts of craft materials and Matilda set to work. She showed amazing talent and completed two castles, one of which was a snow castle.

She became fascinated by a robin in the garden and would watch him any time she appeared. She told me that Jesus had told her that there was a bit in the Bible about birds in Matthew chapter 6 which she had read. When she was sad and "tired in her heart" she would watch "Mr Robin" and draw lovely pictures of him. By this stage she was able to ask Jesus to take "the sad" so that she could receive "happy". She had become used to talking to Jesus and often heard Him say things to her.

In this way her understanding of Him and His love for her and for everyone else was growing.

It became clear that she blamed herself for everything bad that had happened in her life and that of her family. One day she texted that she had a "lot of things in her head" which troubled her. As I could not go to her at the time, I phoned her to chat about it all and find out whether I could help her. It seemed that the things in her head were caused by evil spirits tormenting her, and that Jesus had told her to "tell the lions to stop". She was worried about the lions, so I explained that Jesus was using that name to describe the voices that were annoying her mind, and explained that He had already defeated them for us even though they were trying to make her think that they were in charge. I told her that Jesus is in charge and looking after her. In order to help her to stop being fearful I told her that the lions had no teeth! She laughed at that and told them to "go away like Jesus said". The next day she sent me a picture that she had drawn of the lions. (The drawings are hers but I have overlaid her speech bubbles with printed ones to maintain confidentiality.)

As time went on Jesus grew her up through the years healing her on the way. Her adult-part was thrilled by the creativity which had become so evident in this little one who was part of her.

Alysa's Story

Early on in our meetings, after the child, Alysa, had surfaced from within the adult, I told her the story of Jesus and the lost sheep and I bought her a toy lamb as a present. She identified herself with the lamb, which had to be a "her", and got very upset if she couldn't find her. She referred to herself in the third person and used this toy lamb to express what she was thinking. After our first meeting, whenever Jesus brought her up for ministry, she would ask me, "Do you remember Alysa?" She talked about Alysa as though she were someone apart from her.

The story behind Alysa's abuse was tragic. People had treated her as a thing to be used for their pleasure and amusement. She was totally obedient to them and would do exactly what she was told to do. Everything she did or that was done to her was endured so she could "earn money" to give to the "man". This "man" had promised to find her mummy when he had enough money. Of course, this never materialised. She had been fed on dog scraps, food waste from dustbins, rotting flesh with maggots, or not at all, and so when I gave her food or something to drink, she would consume it as fast as she could for fear it would be given to someone else or to the dog. She was conditioned to be ravenously hungry after any abuse and was likely to eat anything. She had a spirit of malnutrition which we removed.

As she went through various memories, we learnt that, many times, she was not paid "enough" or not at all, and "man" would get angry at her. She was absolutely petrified of him and had a mindset that everything had to be done to earn money and every good deed was to earn money. She was used to obeying without question and initially was always asking me "How much?" It took a long time for her to understand that I did things for her because I loved her and not for payment. Sometimes she had been told she was not "good enough" for the man and they wouldn't give her "much money". She had been told that the only way she could earn the money was if she was running and was caught by the men. She was always running. She was firmly convinced that the "man" was using the money she earned to find her mummy.

The people abusing her had been aiming to rob her of her person-hood. Jesus had pre-empted them, and He told Alysa that He had kept her person-hood and her sense of colour safe, by "using a shiny key". When God uses unexpectedly strange phrases, we respond using the same wording even though we may not understand. In the early days of my knowing her, she was only able to see various shades of grey, void of colour. Alysa had been so abused that she couldn't talk about it. As I watched her draw a lamb with head and arms and legs but without a body because "that bit hurts", my heart was grieved.

After a considerable time in which I gave this little one unconditional love and reassurance along with much prayer, she began to trust me and eventually could say, "Alysa likes Heather" and "Heather likes Alysa". Whenever she talked about things that had happened, she did so through Lamb because she could not identify herself with the distress that she had undergone.

Although she now seemed able to make statements about Alysa and Heather loving each other, she seemed unable to talk about lamb loving Alysa. In some way I think Alysa was finding it difficult to love or accept herself. After some time, she said she wanted to feel love. It was at this point that God "unlocked her person-hood" and quickly she was able to "see love". She described it as "many colours". Then she began to say, very hesitatingly, things like, "I am me". It was as if she was being restored bit by bit away from being a detached thing called Alysa towards being the person called Alysa. It was a truly wonder-filled process. Eventually she was able to say, "I, Alysa, love you, Heather". She became alive and instead of portraying quiet, dead acquiescence, she showed enthusiasm and vitality. Previously she had always said "If you would like me to....". Now she was able to say, "I choose to...".

Over the months Alysa demonstrated a sense of beauty, and wonder at the beauty around her. Through her influence I was encouraged to move into a greater appreciation of the beauty of flowers. She loved to examine them in their different shapes and colours and a visit to a garden centre became her chief source of delight. She took to drawing flowers at every opportunity and, very often, had a message to go with the drawing, messages like, "You will never walk alone", "Praise the Lord" and, after a long time, "Son loves Lamb". These drawings always had a beauty about them, often with gold dots or kisses placed carefully around and within the flower.

Eventually, she was able to draw the lamb with a body, talk in the first person and receive healing directly from Jesus for herself rather than through this toy. She would often place her finger at different places over my face, all the while saying, "love touch, love touch". Her soft toy, "Lamb", was well loved and hugged by the time God had completed healing her.

Alysa, from first knowing Jesus, sang quite ethereally and hauntingly in worship. Sometimes Jesus would speak the words of a song to a child-part and they would sing it and write it out. One such song given to and written by Alysa went as follows,

> Come to me my children
> Let me hold you close
> Come to me my children
> I want to love each most
> I want to show you the wonders
>
> The wonders all around
> The stars that shine in the night sky
> The flowers that colour the ground
>
> The silver in the moonlight
> The gold in the morning sky
> My children why don't you come now
> Why o why o why

Jesus called Alyssa, "the child of innocence", not because she was innocent of evil, but because her character had retained the beauty of innocence despite the atrocities done to her. On the completion of our ministry time with her, Jesus took her to be with Him and enjoy "the flowers that never fade or perish" until such time as He would return her to her adult-part. I have so many happy memories of her and of other child-parts that far outweigh any specifics of their painful memories and emotions.

Miriam and Bekah

Miriam and Bekah were two parts of a young woman who had been badly abused over many years. They manifested at different times.

God brought Miriam first. She was loveable and mischievous, enjoyed hiding in cupboards and sliding down stairs. Although Miriam was extrovert, she was extremely sensitive. She loved sweets and, soon after she came, took sweets one day without asking, but her conscience was so stricken that she was upset and confessed. It took a lot of persuading on my part to reassure her that it didn't make any difference to my love for her. She was terrified of being "hit" because she associated this with complete rejection. She had a sunny disposition, and if ever she was feeling miserable, she would say she needed some more sunshine and would pump at her tummy supposedly pumping in sunshine! When I was shopping with Miriam one day, she chose a white polar bear and, because she liked sweets called "snowies", she decided to call the bear "Snowy". Snowy went everywhere with her in a knapsack. Snowy was a person and had feelings. When Miriam was talking about the bad things that had happened to her, she covered Snowy's ears in case he would hear and become sad. In her eyes Snowy was a soldier who stood for Jesus. Because I am Scottish, Miriam, in identifying with me, developed a great love for Scotland and things Scottish such as a tartan purse and some tartan ribbon. She thought of herself as "Scotland" and, after she heard reference to them in a Scottish song, talked about her mountains and glens. As a bit of fun, I made Snowy a tartan kilt, jacket and soldier's cap. Miriam was delighted and from that point on Snowy was a Scottish soldier. When he was not working, the hat came off. Miriam, herself, had a tartan sash and loved to dance to Scottish music. By the time that Miriam was returned fully healed to her adult-part, Snowy was well travelled and quite the worse for wear!

Bekah surfaced shortly after Miriam. By this time Miriam had persuaded me that she was second in command (after me). Bekah didn't like this one bit as she wanted this position, so she started telling tales about Miriam to show me that Miriam was not fit to be second in command. This turned out to be uncharacteristic of her but, early on, she was suffering from deep rejection and fighting for attention and acceptance, and the demonic spirit within her was driving her into this behaviour. Looking back later it seemed ridiculously funny because Bekah wouldn't hurt a fly, and she turned out to be gentle, caring and self-effacing. Her particular soft toy was a tiny teddy called Barney.

Within a couple of weeks Miriam and Bekah were firm friends and doing their best to care for each other. How they were able to share thoughts and emotions while below the surface remains a mystery to me but is something that has occurred consistently in those who have fragmented person-parts, inner child-parts and prodigals[14], and/or alter egos and core identities[15]. It might be because they are parts of the same person and, therefore, connected in spirit. I have witnessed it occurring consistently and leading to mutual understanding and growing togetherness amongst the child-parts which in turn prepares them for their times of intermingling.

From then on, the true character of the girls surfaced, each being self-effacing and thinking of the other as really special. Each would do anything for the other and each praised the other. Both liked the song "Wind beneath My Wings"[16] believing that her hero was the other. Even to this day my spirit is deeply touched and tears come to my eyes as I listen to this song. These child-parts who had come through so much had such beautiful spirits. Each thought herself not worth much, so it was a continuous job building up confidence in each one.

Miriam loved splashing in puddles, but Bekah thought this was really strange and dirty. However, it became evident that Bekah would like to splash with the gay abandon of Miriam. So, we found her a clean puddle

---

14 Chapter 2.2, p 93
15 Chapter 2.3, p 114
16 Wind beneath My Wings written by Jeff Silbar and Larry Henley 1982. Sung by Bette Midler

and, with a huge smile of delight, she waded through it. For a long time after, Bekah would laugh about splashing in her clean puddle. Miriam, for all her "dare devil" approach to life, would not even consider walking over the rope bridge. Bekah, who was quiet and cautious, loved it and thought of it as her fun. Bekah, though sensitive, had more confidence (a sort of quiet assurance) than Miriam and would quite happily pay in a shop. Miriam was terrified to do so in case she had the wrong money and someone would shout at her.

Miriam discovered that she could win at skittles but always lost at cards. She never wanted to play cards. Because she was fearful of losing, it took a lot of persuading to help her learn to lose happily. She loved hide and seek and invariably fell or got dirty in some way. That was Miriam! When we went for a walk, she loved to draw a map of the route which she then studied from time to time to make sure we were going in the right direction. On one memorable occasion near Christmas time, while walking in a forest, she decided to decorate a tree with our hats and scarves and gloves. Amidst great laughter, I lost my footing on a slope and fell and cut my ear. We had to go to a nearby chemist to get the blood stopped. Miriam was devastated by this and recalled it from time to time. Unlike Miriam, Bekah liked to stay clean but at the same time longed to be able to let go and have fun. She had a serenity about her but worried that she was boring compared to Miriam and it took a long time before she began to understand that she also had qualities which were special.

Both girls were courageous and had beautiful characters. They were loving, caring, sensitive, gentle, generous, kind, wise and full of fun despite the awful things they had experienced. It was as though they were completely untainted by the evil to which they had been exposed or by the ungodly influences of the world around them.

Both loved to worship. Bekah liked to dance and Miriam liked to compose worship songs and jingles. One such was,

> "Jesus is the One we love
> He empowers us from above
> Look to Him, the Bright Morning Light
> Everything's going to be all right."

Miriam was a great story teller and loved to 'phone me and, exaggerate how awful she was finding something. Suddenly she would pause, then giggle and say, "I loves you". Miriam just left things in heaps. Bekah folded everything up as though it was being displayed in a shop. As you can imagine, Miriam's favourite colour was bright yellow. With permission from her adult-part, she painted the inside of a clothes cupboard bright yellow and stuck a Noah's Ark transfer on it. Both had a great love for Jesus and for Jesus' Daddy and would have done anything that He asked of them.

Over the years, we have ministered to many, many child-parts who, despite having suffered greatly, brought us so much joy. To avoid confusion between any child-parts who surfaced within a person, God gave each a special name as they surfaced. His choice of name frequently gave an indication of a specific quality in the child e.g., one little girl whom He called His love child, was named Laleisha, meaning "love blossoms". One, who was called Eve, didn't like her name until He gave her this poem,

> "Eve, Eve, My beautiful Eve
> You are the one My love will never leave
> You are the brightness on a dull and dark day
> You are the one to show many the way
> Because love is the way."

Preparation for Intermingling Two Child-parts belonging to a Person.

The preparation is different for each child-part and is specific to that child-part's needs, abilities, tastes and personality. Jesus always chooses some unique way in which to prepare each part in order to help them look forward to intermingling with each other. Sometimes He tells them of some strength within that they could contribute to the whole. Sometimes they come to know and care for one another to such an extent that they want to share their life together. It is important to spend as much time as is needed with each part to resolve any fears and to help them have healthy relationships, reassuring and preparing each for the intermingling so that each part takes up position with confidence, not holding back nor taking precedence. Being restored into one is an enormous step as each part has been broken off in response to unbearable torment, pain or fear and it takes time, unconditional love and acceptance, growth in confidence etc., for each to leave the learned responses to abuse behind.

Prior to asking God to join two child-parts, we always bound deception and asked that only the truth would be seen. This is because the enemy could interfere at this stage and stop a godly intermingling from taking place. The child-part that emerges after the intermingling of the two parts (the complete mingled part made up of the two) usually can relate some wonderful unique insight into the joining e.g., Jesus taking each by the hand and drawing them together, or twirling with them until they were intermingled, or Jesus winding ribbon round and round them both until they intermingled together. The ways of God are infinite and infinitely beautiful.

Some Reasons for Delay in Joining

- growing the child-part up too fast without the necessary nurture
- resentment on either side
- unequal participation

What follows are accounts, each written by the different child-parts belonging to one person who had been severely abused. In each child-part healing had been completed and the child grown up by Jesus to the age of the next oldest fragmented child-part who, having been healed, was also ready to be intermingled. These descriptions demonstrate how each was prepared by Jesus for this, and the reality of what each felt prior to joining with the other. It illustrates the orderly fashion in which Jesus restores a person to wholeness. As we previously indicated Jesus gave each child a name all of their own to help them believe that they were known and valued. They kept this name until the time of joining with another child-part and then the new combined part would receive a new name and healing would continue. These accounts are written by the child-parts themselves.

Rachel (age 7) (leaving uncorrected the text below as it was written by the child-part)

> "When I came I was 4. I was very scared Jesus gave me two new 'mummys' two good ones because my mummy was bad They showed me that there are good people and that love is not sore but it is kind I want to be loved now Jesus is the only man I know who loves the right way I like him and his daddy I am still a bit scared when someone gets angry but I know now its because they are sore inside I want to join Martha a lot She is so good and helps every one and she is so funny I know she only puts on a show to fool us but everyone knows that is what it is I think shes great Ruth is very wise and gentle I know it will be brill when Jesus joins us together"

(It appears that Rachel hadn't leant yet about punctuation. She had a gentle spirit, was caring, compassionate, forgiving, loving and conciliatory.)

Martha (age 7)

"When Jesus woke me up I was a pretty nasty peese of work he called me incorigable I liked it I always wanted my own way and I always wanted to be boss I never wanted anybody to know the real me now Im second in command and I don't boss anymore cawse Jesus is the boss but he lets everyone pick what they want to do hes great I love Heather and --- but I love Jesus more that's the way it has to be I like being alive now its good fun I like to help everyone now and I try to be good its hard but Im learning Jesus is the best helper out Heather and --- are the next I hope I can do what they do they loved me at the start when I was rotten they never made me make a promise but they lisened to why I couldn't they trusted me and so I lerned to trust them and Jesus I want Rachel and me to be one cause I think she is so good and cares I want to be good to. Happy days ahead"

(Martha was full of fun and liked to help people who were sad or in trouble.)

The Joining of Rachel and Martha to become Deborah

Only after we were certain that Rachel and Martha each believed that they had an important contribution to make, did we ask Jesus to intermingle them. Prior to this we had encouraged each child-part to have a secret sign that confirmed that they really were who they said they were (this was one of the ways that we guarded against deception, copycats, and confusion from intruder spirits – see later[17]). After they were intermingled, we asked the combined part to give the two signs, the one belonging to Rachel and the one belonging to Martha. In this way we ensured that the combined person-part was equally influenced by both Rachel and Martha. The characteristics of each of the previous child-parts always appeared in the combined part, thus making her more

---

17 Page 102

complete. As you can imagine, in a person who has been fragmented, the part of the person that has been left to live life as best they can, does so with only a small fraction of their full potential. Through progressive healing and integration of the child-parts the person is restored to completeness and to wholeness just as they were when created.

Deborah (age 7) (punctuation left uncorrected)

"there was Martha and there was Rachel Jesus brought them both together who is the most important he asked them she is they both said who is the least important me they both said that's good he said you are both the same the three danced together Jesus asked Martha if she wanted to give Rachel a hug and asked Rachel if she wanted a hug they both wanted it Martha asked if Rachel wanted a Heather-hug they both laughed and hugged Rachel hugged Martha and Jesus said that love binds together and then shiney snow fell over us those who God has joined together let no man pull asunder they were one the two became one he gave her a new name Deborah a warrior and a wise counsellor I am very happy and really excited."

(Child-parts hear Jesus extremely easily as they have no worldly distractions so it is never a surprise when they come out with a truth of scripture or use phrases which they otherwise wouldn't have known.)

Joining child-part to adult-part

Once all the child-parts in a person have been healed, restored and progressively intermingled into one, the fully intermingled part is then healed when required during the process of being grown up through the years until the present age of the adult. Time is spent with this intermingled child-part and with the adult-part ensuring they are each truly desiring to become united. Hindrances to joining can include,

- the adult-part not facing reality
- the child-part anxious as to whether the adult-part really wants them
- the adult-part may be afraid that in allowing the child-part to join back into their life they will experience great pain

Once both are happy to join together, they ask God to do this and so He completes the restoration. As previously, we then check that both parts are equally present and content. There is always great rejoicing and gratitude to God.

Chapter 1.4
Other Forms of Fragmented Person-parts and their Restoration

"I pray that the eyes of your heart may be enlightened in order that you may know the hope to which he has called you, the riches of his glorious inheritance in his holy people." Ephesians 1:18

Where the outcome of severe trauma on a person has caused them to fragment in some way other than as a full fragmentation, the approach to healing can be in one of two ways. This is according to which way God thinks is the better for the person, and takes into consideration how comfortable they are with the possibility of allowing their fragmented child-part to surface.

Sometimes a person is afraid of not being in control and so finds it difficult to take a back seat while ministry takes place directly with their fragmented person-part. In such situations, ministry to the fragmented part may be done through the person-part normally on the surface. At a later date if that person becomes confident with the process, they may elect to allow the fragmented part to surface for the remainder of the healing.

On the other hand, a person who has become familiar with the whole concept of fragmentation may choose to allow the fragmented person-part to surface for healing right from the onset of ministry.

The specific difference in healing between the two is that communication can take place directly with any fragmented person-part which surfaces, but has to be done indirectly through the adult with any part that remains below the surface. In each case, there is a reliance on the Holy Spirit for insights and guidance, and in the latter the person-part on top needs to be able to sense what is happening in the fragmented part. This happens through sensing emotions and thoughts that clearly don't seem to belong to them, or though dreams and revelation from God.

Throughout the years that we have been involved in this ministry, God has revealed twelve different ways in which people can become fragmented, each through trauma. As you read through these please don't become overwhelmed with the detail. It is included as a means of enlightening anyone who needs specific understanding about a particular type of fragmentation. I encourage you on first reading to focus on how amazing our God is in His love and compassion for each of us and in His willingness to help us in our times of need.[18]

Healing and restoration of each person-part follows the general pattern outlined in the previous chapter. When discussing characteristics of the other eleven fragmentations I will share any additional specific insights needed for their healing and restoration. Most fragmentations are part of the spirit together with part of the soul but some are part of the soul only.

Partial fragmentation

A partial fragmentation of a person is part of their spirit together with part of their soul. It is caused by fear or terror emanating from someone else and surrounding the person to such a degree that, internally, they withdraw and then go into denial. The fear is not fear as a consequence, but fear of apprehension itself as to what could happen.

---

18 Psalm 46:1; Isaiah 41:10

The partially fragmented part "runs away and hides" as it were behind a partly open door, but is able to peep out and be aware of what is going on around them, and run for safety at the slightest hint of danger. Because of this, some of the memories are known by the person in their conscious mind while others are stored in the partially fragmented part (and in the subconscious mind of the person). Thus, the person may be aware of some of the situations in life that have given rise to this kind of fragmenting. This is different from the fully fragmented part whose memories are all in the unconscious mind of the adult-part and so are not remembered. A person with a fully fragmented child-part may on occasion lose a sense of time passing whereas this doesn't happen with the partially fragmented part.

The partially fragmented part is sensitive to anything negative happening around them, and so the part of the person on the surface can in turn be affected and feel miserable but not know why. Initially, the person-part on the surface may think that the negative emotions belong to them and are arising from something in the present, but if they have used the approaches for inner healing without experiencing any change then it is time to seek God for further insight as to the source. Equally, if they know that the emotional upheaval is either too extreme given their circumstances or has no obvious source then, again, it may be coming from a fragmented person-part within. God will give revelation. It is frequently the case that when a person has a fragmented person-part that any negative emotion, however mild, may tap into that same emotion at a deeper level in the person-part and so appear more intense to the person than circumstances warrant. A partial fragmentation can be called up by the enemy.

Healing and integration of the partial fragmentation is often through the person-part on the surface but there can be exceptions. If the partially fragmented part surfaces with their emotional upheaval and associated memories, the approach in ministry is similar to that for full fragmentation. As the child is healed at one age, they are grown up to the next age at which God wishes to heal. This continues until the partially fragmented part either reaches the age of another fragmented part which has been healed and is ready to be intermingled with them, or until the partially fragmented part reaches the present age of the person, in which case they are intermingled in Jesus' name. If ministry to the partially fragmented part takes place through the person-part usually on the surface, then it may take a little bit longer to ascertain just what is causing the distress and thus be able to address it.

In ministering to people who have been fragmented, we sometimes found that the emotional upheaval in a person-part was affecting the physical health of the whole person. We witnessed this in someone who came to us for help because she couldn't stop being fearful no matter how much she tried, and was suffering from symptoms similar to those of rheumatoid arthritis. As we prayed together, asking God for insight, He revealed that this person had suffered enormous fear as a child and had partially fragmented as a consequence. The fear in the fragmented part had led to her experiencing symptoms like those of rheumatoid arthritis which in turn had affected the adult-part.

We began helping the fragmented child-part to release her fear by asking Jesus to take it away and replace it with His peace. We released her from all demonic fear and closed the door against it, asking Jesus to fill her with His Spirit. Only then did we address the infirmity by commanding it to leave in Jesus' name and go to His feet. The child-part was released from pain and then grown up to the present age of the adult and intermingled back in. The person then found that she was free from pain too. It is important that the person continue walking in her healing by continuing to believe what God has done.

Self-Fragmentation

A self-fragmentation is a fragmentation which has part of the soul and part of the spirit of a person, created as a result of rebellion, perhaps through feeling sheer terror. When someone chooses to rebel deliberately and at the same time deny within themselves that this is what they are doing, they may self-fragment. For much of the time this rebellious self-fragmented part remains dormant but can surface at will, behave badly, and then disappear and the person-part normally on the surface is blamed. Since the person-part normally on the surface lives in self-denial, they can feel they are being unjustly dealt with when punished for what their self-fragmented part did. The truth is that deep within they know that they are responsible.

Self-fragmented parts, because they are just under the surface, are aware of what is going on in the person's life, and so during ministry there are no hidden memories to address, only rebellion. One example was a six-year-old boy whose daddy had left the family home. Because he didn't want to get hurt again, he had chosen to hide away by fragmenting and going into self-denial. Any time that this part came to the surface, he was angry and rebellious.

Using a Partial Fragmentation to enable Self-fragmentation

A person who has a partially fragmented part, and later on finds life overwhelmingly tough, may choose to abdicate their place in life by forcing the partially fragmented child-part to take their place. This is rebellion and leads to the person-part who has been on the surface becoming a self-fragmented part.

This had happened in someone who came to us for ministry because she was stressed that in recent times, she hadn't been able to do her job. Although a cook by profession she could no longer remember how to cook.

As we talked with and befriended her, a timid fragmented person-part (initially the adult person-part but who had self-fragmented so as to avoid taking responsibility) occasionally came to the surface but disappeared at the slightest sign that someone else might be coming near. One day while out walking along the shore we saw the lady and realised that her adult person-part (now a self-fragmented part) was on the surface. However, as soon as she saw us, she disappeared and her partial fragmented child-part surfaced once again, recognising us from ministry.

Over time, the part that was hiding from life (the self-fragmented part) came to talk to us more frequently and we learnt that this was the part that normally cooked. She had chosen to opt out of life so as to avoid being at work because her boss had piled the responsibility of his post onto her as his junior causing her great stress. In opting out she had forced her fragmented child-part, a child who didn't know how to cook, to remain on the surface. Because she lived in self-denial, she hadn't been able to understand why she could no longer cook.

Happily, over time this lady received healing through the ministry of the Holy Spirit.

Slumbering Spirits

A slumbering spirit is a fragmentation of part of the the soul and part of the spirit of a person which has opted out of life by going to sleep. In contrast to self-fragmented parts, slumbering spirits remain buried until such time as God brings them to the surface for restoration.

A slumbering spirit may be created by a person who chooses to ignore what has become emotionally or spiritually unbearable for them. For example, if a person is suffering from emotional pain like unfaithfulness in marriage, they may dump their rejection on a part of them which they separate from and then choose to live in self-denial, as though nothing is wrong. Such a person has a deep need to experience and receive love but finds it difficult as they have "shut down" their ability to receive emotionally.

This is rebellion against life. When anyone receives revelation that they have a slumbering spirit, they need to repent i.e., choose to turn away from self-denial and acknowledge the truth of what has happened so that they can receive healing. Truly, they are as one who says, "I was once in darkness, now my eyes can see".[19] As we walk with Jesus, we are continually being brought out of the darkness that has pervaded so many areas of our lives. This is another aspect of Isaiah 61:1ff.

It is possible, but extremely unlikely, for a person to have more than one slumbering spirit. Instead, each succeeding trauma, having a similar effect on the person, puts the person-part even more soundly asleep. Since a person's spirit can sense something is wrong, even when the person may not be consciously aware of it, a slumbering spirit may be created or, if already present, go deeper into sleep, without the person realising this is happening. An example of this was someone who realised suddenly that over recent weeks she had been feeling less and less alert, as though her mind was increasingly opting out of thinking. It felt like too much of an effort to try to think things through, and she was losing her ability to concentrate and remember things. However, she struggled on and eventually succeeded in overcoming the lethargy.

Years later, the reason for her earlier struggle emerged when she explored it with the help of the Holy Spirit. She learnt that as a baby, a part of her had gone to sleep because of perceived rejection, and any rejection throughout her life had caused this slumbering spirit to go into a deeper and deeper sleep. When, unknown to her, her husband had an affair with another woman, her spirit had sensed what was happening and the already deeply slumbering spirit had gone into an even deeper sleep to the point where she had found it difficult to think and recall. Since the slumbering spirit was linked to her spirit, the increasing lethargy had been affecting the whole person.

Slumbering spirits are usually brought to the surface for healing. As they gradually awaken and surface, the emotional pain within will also be felt by the rest of the person.

---

19   I was Once in Darkness, Joan Parsons, 1978, Thankyou music

While God is healing and restoring a slumbering spirit, so that the person can participate in life again, He will do so slowly, growing the slumbering spirit a little at a time and stopping to reinforce healing until they reach the present age of the other part. Slumbering spirits appear to be lazy, lackadaisical about life, refusing to think for themselves and may opt to sleep again because they do not want to face further pain. However, since they are strong-willed, patient and supportive love encourages them to resist opting out of life by sleeping.

Frequently we had to command the spirit of death to leave. If the person has been "caged", this spirit of death must be removed by Jesus before any slumbering spirit can be restored.

Sometimes what appears to be a slumbering spirit may be something else, e.g., a spirit of Ahab affecting a person which can cause drug-like sleepiness. In satanic ceremonies a person can be induced into sleep through a spirit of dizziness or through trance when subjected to satan's "fire".

Damage to the Soul

The soul, the spirit and the body are inextricably linked and so when something affects one it affects all. The source of an issue may be stored in one, two, or in all three. I want now to highlight three ways in which the soul, but not the spirit, is fragmented by hurt and trauma. These are Semi-Fragmentation, Divided Soul and Torn Soul. The first and second of these are created by self as a defence mechanism whereas the third is directly caused by hurt from others.

Semi-Fragmentation

Some people cope with painful emotions, pressures and stresses by unintentionally compartmentalising their soul (but not their spirit) into two parts, one part gathering pain and distress while the other lives on in self-denial as though nothing has happened. This is called a semi-fragmentation.

God likens the part of the soul, with the pressures dumped in it, to a knapsack carried on the person's back. Those who shrug off the effects of pressures impinging upon them generally hold to the philosophy, "that's life". They appear to cope abnormally well despite a huge amount of pressure, much of which comes from circumstances or from the people around them. Unfortunately, although they appear to cope well in such circumstances, these build up within them in a part of their soul that has become a dumping ground and is like a dead thing without spirit and life.

This part of the soul is missing from involvement in everyday life, leaving a gap in the soul. The Lucifer spirit[20] is quick to seize the opportunity and occupy that place. Remember - our enemy is opportunistic, prowling around seeking whom he may devour[21]. From within the soul, he then gives abnormal strength to the person so that they appear to be resilient and able to cope with increasing amounts of pressure. The irony of Lucifer's presence is that he attracts more and more problems across the path of his host at the same time as giving them false strength. Lucifer spirits may also cause mood swings within the person and bring up negative emotions from the past. Because the person is not resolving any of this with God's help, they become increasingly vulnerable to the sheer weight of pressure on the part of their soul used for storage. When it suits his purposes, the Lucifer spirit will withdraw his input and the person will suddenly go into overload and no longer cope. The song, "Pack up your troubles in your old kit bag and smile, smile, smile"[22] describes this well, particularly when you consider the line, "while you've a Lucifer to light your fag...." Although the "Lucifer" in the song represents a box of matches,

---

20   Unveiling our True Identity in Christ, Chapter 2.6
21   1 Peter 5:8
22   Pack up your troubles, George Henry Powell (1880 – 1951), pseudonym George Asaf

God pointed out this song as relevant to our understanding of semi-fragmentation. It is a good representation of the spirit of Lucifer because he lies in wait, strengthening a person to take on more and more pressure, and then suddenly withdraws that strength and the person experiences burn-out.

God encourages us to talk out our stresses with Him and let Him take the burdens,

> *"Cast your cares on the Lord and he will sustain you; he will never let the righteous be shaken."* Psalm 55:22

A sign that this type of fragmentation may be present in a person occurs when, suddenly, they can no longer cope as they did previously with daily stresses. They may feel as though they are carrying a huge weight around on their backs even when nothing seems to warrant it. Once a person understands what has been happening and acknowledges that their way of dealing with problems was not right, they can repent and, in Jesus' name, ask Him to remove the back pack (the build-up of pressures and stresses) and the spirit of Lucifer, and heal their soul (Psalm 23). The two parts of the soul will knit together as the person walks in truth, dealing honestly with each pressure or pain as it comes.

The Divided Soul

When a person has two separate goals and the pull of each goal is strong, their soul may split into two equal parts pulling in opposite directions. Each of these halves to the person's soul remains associated with the whole of the person's spirit. Each has a very strong will and knows that there is another part to their thinking but chooses to ignore it as far as possible. Both parts may be near the surface, each uppermost at different times, thus causing the person to alternate between one kind of behaviour and another. In his letter James calls this, "double mindedness"[23].

People can be double-minded for all kinds of reasons such as addiction to alcohol, gambling, drugs and pornography. When an addict wants to give the impression that they are living free of any addiction, in refusing to face the truth they may inadvertently split their soul in two, one part living in denial of the addiction, and so having deception at the core; the other part satisfying the driven-ness to addiction. Since each has a strong will, it takes determination within the person, along with the grace of God, to live an honest open life and get free. There is likely to be a spirit of addiction associated with it which will need to be rejected. The tendency to addiction may have been passed on from a previous generation.

A divided soul can occur for other reasons. Some people, in choosing to avoid feeling deep pain and hurt because it is expected of them, cause their soul to be divided. One half holds the pain and hurt while the other half lives in denial. Others, who believe that not harbouring a grudge against another is achieved through denying the pain, may resort to this way of coping. As they become practiced in this form of denial, so that it becomes a habit, they may even convince themselves that they never feel anger or rage at injustice against themselves, and that they never feel bitter. Sadly though, some may, in the privacy of their own home, play out their anger on family members or even be planning for the day when they will take revenge. Evil spirits can be attracted to this emotional upheaval and feed in more negativity.

On one occasion during ministry, God illustrated how the two parts of a divided soul operate independently by using the yin and the yang symbolism[24]. This was merely to aid understanding and not in any way to affirm links with the occult.

---

23 James 1:8
24 Yin and yang – Wikipedia https://images.app.goo.gl/6Vtga6eCRtpDv7qq8

Together the two "halves" of the symbol show completeness (a circle in which the two parts of the divided soul together represent the whole soul). The white half with a black dot can be used to represent the part of the divided soul that lives in denial of the truth. This person-part presents a good front (the white) but has  deception (self-denial) in their heart (the black dot). The other half is represented by the black part with the white dot because it appears bad in some way, perhaps through negative emotional outbursts caused by harbouring pain and hurt. Despite appearances, this part has a good heart, is honest, and faces the true facts (the white dot). Whenever the person is further hurt or pressured and stressed, their emotional responses are quickly dispatched into the "bad part" and the "good part" thinks they're coping well. This leads to more deception in the "good part" and to an increasing build-up of anger, hatred, bitterness and resentment in the "bad part". A divided soul may appear to be similar to a self-fragmentation but the cause for each and consequent outcome is different.

In a divided soul the "bad" half that has all the negative emotions dumped on them can often be resentful of the half doing the dumping. In their thinking this other half is "Mr (Miss) Goody Two Shoes". Accordingly, they may not want anything to do with this part but choose a life of hatred and revenge, one which Jesus warned us about[25] and which gives a foothold to evil spirits. Because the "good" half has to keep up appearances, rather than display unacceptable emotions they dump it on their other soul part ("bad" half). Over time this "bad" part may collect anger and hatred from choice. It is important always to remember that God loves each part of the person, sees the heart of the person no matter what appearances look like, and wants to help.

---

25 Matthew 5:21-24.

Healing

Those who seek help because they are struggling with an inner drive towards behaviour which is unacceptable to them usually do not understand why this is so. Before any restoration can take place, they need to be affirmed with consistent unconditional love, and given a lot of understanding and support by the person to whom they have gone for help. Only when they feel safe, and know that they will not be shamed, will they acknowledge the depth and destructive nature of what they are trying to suppress. Further gentle questioning and discussion can uncover the root causes and gradually the person can begin to understand what is happening. At this stage it can be given a name – divided soul – and the explanation offered. Usually by then the person feels relief in recognising and understanding why there has been inner turmoil, what has caused it and how to resolve it.

At this point, the person readily recognises and acknowledges the deception that they have been living under, and is willing to renounce it. Facing the truth may give rise to fear that they will be rejected by God and others so they need wise and patient affirmation. They may also be afraid that the hidden emotions will overwhelm them when released. Reassurance can be offered through affirming that God takes them at a pace that they can manage and that, with gentleness and grace, He replaces the negativity with His love and peace. The goal is that the person becomes internally united, of one mind and heart, that of Christ.

Only after the "good" half has rejected all deception, and is willing to allow the other half to surface enough to be restored, can ministry to the "bad" half proceed. When near the surface this part can be so full of anger, hatred and venomous intent, coupled with unpleasant accusations about everyone around them, including the one seeking to help, that it can frighten the other "good" part. This is especially so if they have been walking with God and living in the truth of scripture for years. Any onslaught may be exaggerated by the effect of the demonic on the divided soul, and requires the person helping to continue offering unconditional acceptance, without allowing themselves to be drawn into the negativity and manipulation. This uncharacteristic behaviour is alternated with profound apologies and accompanying distress from the other "bad" part. The person helping needs to be confident in God and consistently stable so as to facilitate the healing. Frequently, gentle inner healing is central to restoration of the "bad" part.

It can be an extremely painful and confusing time for the "good" part of the person until they understand what is coming from the demonic and what is coming from the hurting emotions of the "bad" part, and that despite appearances this other part has a good heart. The demonic has to be rejected in Jesus' name, the hurting emotions and thoughts expressed and released to Jesus and His peace received, while at the same time strengthening the "good" part as they seek to support and encourage their other half. On any occasion when a "bad" part appears at the surface that part needs to feel that same acceptance and love as the "good" part. Only through knowledge of the love of Jesus for them, and through feeling truly accepted and understood, and their hurt feelings supported, can they allow themselves the freedom to let go of their "ammunition". All this takes sensitivity, patience and consistent support on the part of those doing ministry. Little by little the hurting part can be helped to hand over the negative feelings to Jesus and become less angry and more able to receive the love that Jesus is offering. As we progress in ministry there will be deliverance from time to time as the Holy Spirit leads. Gradually this part becomes free of all demonic and negativity and is able to bring their thinking under control and be filled with the peace of Jesus. Once the two parts are living in the truth and free of the negativity, they will merge as one, bound in the love of Jesus.

The Story of Penny who had a Divided Soul

Having been hurt and rejected by her mother Penny perceived rejection from everyone around her. This led to part of her "dying" and to fragmentation of her personality, parts one and two. Part one lived in denial, not knowing Jesus and with low self-image and no ability to decide for herself. She thought of herself as bad, stupid and unloved. According to her, part two was "dead" but, in actual fact, when she was allowed to surface it turned out that she knew Jesus, had a lively spirit and was a decision maker. As ministry progressed and part one came to know Jesus, part two became worried because she thought that this might exclude her in some way.

Once ministry to both parts was under way, it was of particular interest to me that the two child-parts each lived in awareness of one another's needs and desires. I had a colouring book which I offered to part one, asking her if she would like to choose a picture to colour. This she did and then, using her right hand, coloured in only half of each part of it. Her colouring was quite precise and not in any way a scribble, but she appeared to have left the colouring incomplete. Later, I gave the same colouring book to part two of the person and invited her to choose any picture to colour. She turned the pages until she came to the picture that part one had been colouring and then, using her left hand, coloured the rest of the picture so that it was complete.

On another occasion when I gave part one something to eat, she used her right hand to eat half of the meal. She told me the other half was for the "dead" one.

When ministry to each was complete and they asked Jesus to join them together, the combined child-part described it as Jesus, "squashing them together".

It seems that, unlike other fragmentations which are a homogeneous part of the whole, a divided soul is the soul sliced down the middle to give a right part and a left part and what's in the one is not in the other.

Torn Soul

A torn soul may occur when a person feels "ripped apart" by another, often as the result of harsh treatment,

> *"Lord my God, I take refuge in you; save and deliver me from all who pursue me, or they will tear me apart like a lion and rip me to pieces with no one to rescue me."* Psalm 7:1-2

It is a tearing apart of the emotions, often at an early age, and affects only a small part of the soul, not half as in the divided soul. Whether a person's emotions are ripped apart or not may depend on the severity of the hurt, the sensitivity of the person, and the context in which the injury is inflicted. It is as though the person has been ravaged and torn apart, devastated, worthless, insecure, insignificant, and useless.

This can happen as a result of the confusion that arises through contradictory messages being given to the child e.g., through sexual abuse being described as love, or severe spanking as a means of "getting the bad out of the child" being legitimized as the outcome of the parent's love. Profound fear of punishment may birth within the child a fear of doing the wrong thing to the extent that the child backs off while protesting innocence over every mishap. For example, if a parent were to say their arm was sore, that child might back off out of fear of being held responsible. Such a child may crave love to the point of continuously coming forward for it only to back off out of fear when the desired closeness is coming, or they may constantly be making statements like, "don't leave me", and be clingy. One person I knew was so filled with fear that she found it impossible to admit that she had no money for food. This was because she thought that in acknowledging her need, she was demonstrating failure on her part which would lead to an angry response and punishment.

When a person has a torn soul, gentle loving understanding and empathy help the person to verbalise their pain, their feelings and their thoughts, and to acknowledge the sin of the abuser. Such a person needs the love of the Father to heal, and this can begin as the person responds to God's promptings to talk about their fears and any injustices in their lives, and to release them to Him so that they can receive His peace. Once the person experiences peace, then they are able to forgive[26] from their heart. Sometimes, God may bring up a memory which in turn leads to the surfacing of deep hurting emotions. The route to freedom always begins with honest dialogue with God and releasing pain. The gentle consistent and unchanging love that we ourselves have received from the Father can touch the person and help them to trust Him. He alone "knits the soul", restoring it (Psalm 23:3).

One person found that, when her torn soul was healed and intermingled back in, an eating disorder and a drinking habit, which had previously been sorted, returned. She took authority over her soul and commanded it in Jesus' name to come into order and the problems stopped. This demonstrates that healing which has occurred in the person who has a torn soul does not automatically change fleshly desires in the part that was torn. In this it is like other fragmented parts which need to be near the surface to receive healing. Watchman Nee writes, "The soulish system is a power in itself."[27] It is good to pray,

> *"May God Himself, the God of peace, sanctify me through and through."* 1 Thessalonians 5:23

Captive Spirits

A captive spirit is a fragmented part of a person which has been taken and held captive in some way by the enemy. A person can have a captive spirit or be a captive spirit. Although called captive spirits, these person-parts are fragmented in soul as well as spirit, sometimes for generational reasons, sometimes from conception or occurring later in life. Even

---

26 Stop feeling angry or resentful towards someone
27 The Latent Power of the Soul, Watchman Nee, Christian Fellowship Publishers, 1972

when a fragmented person-part is in captivity, they are still linked in spirit to the person to whom they belong Thus, when a captive spirit is tormented in some way, the torment is felt by the other part of the person for no apparent reason, often causing a sense of oppression. At the same time as a person-part is taken captive, an evil spirit is left in exchange e.g., Jezebel, Ahab, a spirit of torment etc. Consequently, the person can be influenced by the same torment. Sometimes they can feel they are absent from life somehow. One person described herself as, "not being at home".

Some Reasons why a Person may have a Captive Spirit

A person-part may be taken captive because of trauma, some form of occult involvement, or rebellion against God whether it is their own or that of someone in a previous generation. Any foothold that the enemy has is only because he is an opportunist. More than one person-part from any one person may be taken captive but there must be separate footholds for each.

An example arising from the influence of the occult emerged with one client who had come for ministry because she was experiencing strong demonic opposition to her proposed marriage. As a child she had suffered from eczema and been taken by her father to a woman who did charms. In so doing the father had unwittingly placed his daughter under the influence and covering of the woman. God revealed to us during ministry that the woman who had charmed the eczema had been a witch and that on that visit she had used the opportunity to fragment the child, causing part of her soul and spirit to be made captive to satan.[28] Happily, the lady was released from captivity and married soon afterwards.

A foothold, that allows the enemy to take a fragmented person-part captive, may have been given in a previous generation but will only be used in this way by the enemy when it suits. Sometimes it can be generations

---

28 Page 94

later as was the case for someone who came for ministry because she was overwhelmed by fear. We discovered that in a previous generation her family had practiced witchcraft thereby giving a foothold to the enemy. Consequently, while in the womb a part of her had been fragmented and taken captive, accompanied by a curse that this part would never see the light. When we broke the curse in Jesus' name, she was greatly comforted by "seeing" an angel. We then asked Jesus to release her captive spirit and remove the Jezebel spirit left in her place. He told us that He would keep the rescued captive for two weeks before returning her to the person and joining them together because that part needed comfort, help, tenderness and understanding as well as deliverance.

Generally, when a child is dedicated to satan at birth or soon after it is only part of the spirit and soul of that child or of selected offspring in future generations that is taken captive. This is sufficient to allow satan access to that person's life so as to torment them mercilessly. However, if a baby or young child is wholly dedicated to satan by their parents, then that child can become a captive spirit as opposed to having part of their spirit made captive. What this means is that practically all their spirit is made captive, and, therefore, in satan's domain. The whole spirit cannot be held in captivity as this would mean there was no part of the person's spirit left in the body and the body would cease to function in the physical world. For this reason, a very little part of the person's spirit is left in the body but this is complemented by a demonic spirit such as Jezebel. This means that the person may appear to be "Jezebellic" in nature while being tormented by this spirit.

A Glimpse into the Mystery surrounding Captive Spirits

When ministering to a person with a captive spirit, God often reveals exactly what has happened in the spiritual realm and what He is doing to free the captive. Such captivity takes place in the spiritual world, and cannot be fully understood at a cerebral level, so we have to choose whether to follow Jesus in faith. As I have mentioned previously, we take great care through our discernment to check every step in all that appears to be taking place. Confirmation of the reality of what is revealed to us about the torture and subsequent restoration of captives comes each time when, after a captive spirit is returned to the person, the person feels "themselves" more at peace and no longer tormented.

When a fragmented person-part is fleeing, they may see several "doors" but only one will be lit up. To the fragmented part this appears to be the door to safety but it is the one that satan plans for them to go through and although it appears to lead to peace and freedom it actually leads to captivity in some form or other.

Sometimes, the child-part is kept in a cage of some sort, maybe amongst rows of cages alongside the captive spirits of others. At other times the captive spirit may be kept isolated and in distress in a hole. Some sleep. Some cry and shout. Some spit. Some are subdued. Sometimes two captives take a dislike to one another. One captive continually spat at another who was being repeatedly thrown into a corner by demonic and was themselves very quiet. Torment is added to torment. There are an endless number of ways through which the enemy chooses to torment a person through their captive spirit.

The pain that the captive spirits experience from being subjected to such torment is very severe, and so when they are told that having a "monster" (a demonic spirit) would lessen the pain they often agree and accept a monster. Too late they find out that things only get worse. They learn not to trust but to fend for themselves, sometimes taking revenge for their own pain on another. This is the reality of satan's domain.

A captive spirit can put layers and layers of deception, like blankets, over themselves to hide. If they have served satan out of ignorance, and then later come to know Jesus, choosing to follow Him and rejecting everything to do with satan, this cloak can be used temporarily by God to hide the fact that the captive has changed from serving satan to serving

God. This gives time for the captive to become settled in following Jesus before any cloak of deception is removed and satan finds out.

On occasion, a cloak of deception may be left in the person by satan in exchange for a child-part being taken captive. When Jesus was rescuing one captive spirit and we were removing the cloak of deception from the person in Jesus' name, a spirit of witchcraft was uncovered. The enemy had intended that this spirit would never be found. It was responsible for imitating the ailment affecting the person which had been accepted as a genuine physical illness. The cloak of deception was also influencing the person in their thinking, causing confusion and creating a type of daze that was hindering progress in ministry.

A cloak of deception may be left where the person is important to satan for his purposes or where he wants to hinder progress in ministry towards freedom for the person. He sometimes uses it as a deceptive cover over a video (a false set of memories) within a person in an attempt to put ministry counsellors off track and keep them going round in circles without any fruitfulness (chapter 1.5, page 108).

Restoration of a Captive Spirit

The miraculous news is that Jesus came to set the captives, all the captives, free. He, alone, can enter satan's domain because He has defeated him at the Cross and He alone in His love can rescue the tormented,

> *"The Spirit of the Lord is upon Me, Because He has anointed Me To preach the gospel to the poor; He has sent Me to heal the brokenhearted, to proclaim liberty to the captives and recovery of sight to the blind, To set at liberty those who are oppressed;"* Luke 4:18 NKJV

Prior to a captive spirit being released we can help them through prayer. Because they often feel isolated, we can ask Jesus to surround them with a bubble of love. As the love soaks in it breaks the power of the isolation.

Since a captive spirit is vulnerable to confusion and attack from those around them, we can lessen the effects of this on the captive by asking Jesus to put His armour on them.

While in captivity any demonic that is tormenting the captive child will, through the child-part, affect and influence the adult. It may torment in some specific way, or even try to influence the adult into leaving ministry. We can pray, asking Jesus to break all control from every source to do with any demonic. A canopy may be placed between the emotions of the adult and the child fragmentation while healing is in process.

Only Jesus can rescue captive spirits and He usually holds them for two or three weeks while they are being delivered and healed before restoring them to where they belong. Even so, after the person-part has been returned to the person, they may not be intermingled immediately so that the person can get used to the new feelings. Occasionally after rescuing a captive, Jesus may keep that captive spirit for years rather than return them to an adult who would reject their captive spirit again. This is to prevent the captive from falling into the hands of satan once more. Any time up until merging, a fragmented part can be removed again by God but also by satan if the person gives him an opening.

Jesus sometimes intercepts satan when he is about to take a fragmented person-part captive, and keeps that part of the person Himself for years, until the time comes for the total healing of the person. This is because it is part of His healing purpose and part of His overall plan for that person for the future. An example was Lalisha, the "love child", mentioned in the previous chapter.

Examples showing the Variety and Uniqueness of Captivity and Subsequent Restoration

One of the captive spirits, who had been rescued and returned to the person to whom she belonged, was taken back into captivity because the adult-part wanted to remain sick so as to get attention. Jesus told her that He would free her captive spirit once again but only if she wanted to be made whole, because He would not allow the child to be taken captive repeatedly. He freed the captive spirit and continued to hold her safe, waiting for when the adult would welcome her. This was so that neither the captive spirit nor the person would be tormented. Jesus is so merciful,

> *"Then they cried out to the Lord in their trouble, And He saved them out of their distresses. He sent His word and healed them, and delivered them from their destructions."* Psalms 107:19-20

Another adult wanted to be well but also liked to draw attention to herself by not eating properly. This posed a problem because the captive part wanted to eat. However, the adult-part had a good heart and was a fighter and so, with God's grace, overcame her wrong desires.

One cage had a covering which Jesus had used to conceal it. In this cage there were two child-parts, both from the same person. One was pre-birth, there as a result of fear because her parents had been arguing. The other was there because she had rebelled, saying to herself, "that's enough" and had fragmented. This second one was really a self-fragmentation and she should have gone through that particular "door" but, in rebellion, she chose to go through another and so ended up in captivity. We prayed, asking Jesus to return her. He did so and she returned as a self-fragmented person-part who then had to repent and be healed before being intermingled back with the adult-part.

Captive spirits may invite "monsters" in because they are told that it will reduce the pain, but it never does. Having "monsters" does, however, hold back other "monsters". One child was in a large barred cage, lying sleeping in the middle so that the "monsters" couldn't get at her.

While in captivity, because one child had been suffering at the hands of a "monster" sent to attack her by another captive, she retaliated by sending her "monster" to attack back.

One child captive who was held in a cage was upset by the crying of a baby in the next cage and was told that if they swapped cages the crying would stop. They swapped cages but the crying continued. Thinking that it would bring her release she invited in rebellion, hate and anger.

Each time that Jesus showed us in the spirit how He was rescuing a captive spirit, He used a series of graphic pictures and words in demonstration of His faithful persevering love. An example of this was seen in His rescue of the captive spirit belonging to the child who had been charmed by the witch.[29] While ministering to this person we had asked Jesus to go and free her and to remove whatever had been left in her place in the remaining part. As we waited quietly, I heard the words, "through wind and hail and fire, through storm" and, while I was wondering what these words meant, in the spirit I saw Jesus making His way through very deep snow on snow shoes, His body bent in the effort. After what seemed like a long time, but was only five minutes, I witnessed Him reaching a kind of log cabin and going inside. He came out carrying a child on His back and made the return journey through the snow. A while later, I heard the words, "dry land" by which I understood that Jesus and the child were safely out of enemy territory. Then I heard the word, "Siberia" (a symbol of captivity in isolation). After I explained everything to those present, we waited quietly again for God to reveal more. I heard the words, "clap your hands, Daddy's coming home". I was puzzled by this and wondered if they referred to some trauma in childhood where the person had felt deserted by her daddy but then had happily welcomed him home. However, one of the others who was praying heard the word, "witch" and so we realised that what I had heard referred to the time when this person had been taken by her daddy to the woman who did charms. The father had been told to leave his daughter and come back later. This seemed to be the child's

---

29 Page 88

response when her daddy came for her. After this healing the young woman no longer had demonic opposition to her marrying.

Some captive spirits are not locked away in a cage but are left free so that they can come and go as they wish or as commanded by satan. These are usually fragmented person-parts that are captive because of rebellion and do not need to be locked up because they will return of their own accord. Where satan knows the captive spirit will obey him, he sends the captive to create havoc at designated times. In one instance satan used a captive child to go and light fires for him.

Captive spirits of two people may be placed, each in the other. For example, a mother's captive spirit may be placed in the daughter and the daughter's in the mother. When a captive spirit is released from someone and returned to the person to whom they belong, we need to cut in Jesus' name any ungodly soul and spirit ties between that captive spirit and the person in whom they were held captive, and pray that what belongs to each be returned to them. Most captive spirits are grown up within their adult-part after return.

Where there is a captive spirit and a slumbering spirit they may fight. The following is an example of how this was played out within ministry and demonstrates the strong mindedness of slumbering spirits. This slumbering spirit had been caused early on in the womb and God had grown her up to nine months but then stopped. At this point we were told that there was a fragmented person-part who had been taken captive by satan at nine months of age, and a spirit of Jezebel left in her place. While Jesus was returning the captive spirit to the person, we broke any ungodly soul and spirit ties between the captive spirit and satan in Jesus' name, and asked God to remove the Jezebel spirit. Even though Jesus had returned this captive to the person and she ought to have been free, she appeared to be in some sort of "cage" but the door was not locked. She was cold and lifeless and needed love to warm her up and bring her to life, and then encouragement to come out. We suggested to the person, whose captive spirit she was, that she offer unconditional love and reassure her that she wanted her back in her life. Still, the captive remained in her "cage". Eventually, we discovered that the slumbering spirit was threatening the newly released captive by telling her that if she came out of the "cage" she would once again be taken captive by satan. The slumbering spirit had positioned herself across the door of the "cage" in which the captive part was lying. After we understood what was happening, we were able to resolve it by asking Jesus to intervene, preventing the captive spirit from hearing the slumbering spirit taunt her, and reassuring both.

Once each was ready, Jesus intermingled the slumbering spirit and the captive spirit and then grew them up as one. This demonstrates how complicated the process of ministry can be and also the incredible changes for good that happen in a person's life as a consequence.

Personal Fragmentation

The Psalmist writes,

> *"Even when bad things happen to the good and godly ones, the Lord will save them and not let them be defeated by what they face."* Psalms 34:19

Sometimes, in the face of extreme and deliberate ongoing evil torment, which God knows would destroy a person completely if they were not in some way protected, He creates a fragmentation to take the abuse before it begins. As well as enabling the person to carry the burden of repeated extreme abuse, which might otherwise destroy them, it safeguards awareness at the core of their being that God loves them, protecting knowledge of Him and His truth. He gave us the name "personal fragmentation" to describe this.[30]

---

30 Page 32

When God fragments a person, forming a personal fragmentation, He ensures that the fragmented part created by Him is at the surface prior to the torment so as to take the full force of it. Then He interchanges the two parts, bringing the other part to the surface. In this way He prevents part of the person from becoming increasingly fragmented as time goes by. It is like an "upside-down" fragmentation.

It is not that God wants to break up a person by fragmenting them in soul and spirit, but that there are occasions when He knows that there will be repeated traumas in that person's life that could result in progressively more and more of them becoming fragmented because of the need to survive. This could lead to a situation in which the person may hardly be able to function at all and His truth be completely lost to them. Since the part fragmented by God faces the trauma, the other part, which will be brought to the surface after the trauma to live life, has no awareness of what has happened nor of the emotional pain and distress that has taken place.

During restoration, the personal fragmentation part has no memories of what has happened until God shines the light of His truth on them. This contrasts with what we know of other forms of fragmentation which retain conscious memories of specific abuses. As we minister, the full horror of what has happened and its effects on the person-part are revealed. At the end of each session of ministry to the fragmented part, the other part surfaces again vaguely aware of what has happened. As we discuss what has taken place, they are able to recall more and will often add detailed descriptions of events and feelings of the fragmented child-part that weren't fully revealed to us. They have amazing insights into the works of darkness because they have seen them first-hand in the spirit.

If a person has many fragmentations, any personal fragmented part may be the last in the sequence to be healed. This "end of the road" fragmented person-part has been profoundly traumatized because they have nowhere to "dump" any overload: no way of using self-deceptive or self-protecting measures. When God shines His light on what has happened, the accompanying raw emotions that surface are unlike anything else that I have ever experienced. Absolute sheer torment causes the person's face to contort in a way that resembles that of a gargoyle sometimes seen on church buildings. It is heart-wrenching to be alongside such pain, and many times I have cried out to God for mercy, but the truth has to be revealed before the person can become totally free, and so that the enemy's control over the person ceases. God ministers in the most amazing way and, extreme as the trauma is, the person-part is able to receive full healing quickly and completely. Although they may remember what they have been through they will never suffer trauma relating to it again.

Through creating a personal fragmentation in a person, not only does God safeguard the person from complete destruction but, because this personal fragmentation is managed by God, the absolute truth of God's love does not become tainted by exposure to wrong influences in life. Knowing the truth sets us free.[31]

Once this personal fragmentation has been released from the trauma in their life, God takes the person step by step through their life, up to the present, shining the light of His truth on each aspect. Like other fragmented person-parts on this journey, this part does not know anything about their life beyond the point they have reached until further revelation occurs. When they reach events that have already been revealed and worked through by one of the other fragmentations there is a passing through them without trauma. Only those abuses which have never been seen and processed previously by other person-parts are ones that need to be worked through by the personal fragmentation.

Example of Healing a Personal Fragmented Part

This lady came for help because she was in great distress at not being able to do her work. As we explored with her what was happening, we

---

31   John 8:32.

learnt that she had a habit of counting before doing a task because she believed this was necessary in order to accomplish it. We discovered that this counting was bringing on hypnotic trance which was acting like self-hypnosis and interfering with her being able to do her work. It took several weeks to unravel what had happened in her life to cause this.

As a child she had been subjected to fear-provoking events aimed at destroying her mental health. On several occasions she had witnessed Electroconvulsive Therapy (E.C.T.) being administered to her mother and then been subjected to the same treatment. This treatment was not being used for medical reasons but with wicked, evil intentions.

Before she witnessed any of this God had created a personal fragmentation in her so that only this part would experience the full scale of the traumatic events. If He had not taken this step she would possibly have been broken up into several parts, because of the repeated trauma, and unable to function in life. Instead, she had continued in life with no conscious knowledge of what had happened to her as a child and it was only recently that she had been unable to do her work.

After God had released her personal fragmented part from all her trauma and restored her back to where she belonged, she walked free, able to work once again. What an amazing ministry with a miraculous outcome!

Chapter 1.5
Fragmentations which do not Belong to the Person or are False

"Trust in the Lord with all your heart and lean not on your own understanding; in all your ways submit to him, and he will make your paths straight."
Proverbs 3: 5-6

It is important to be alert at all times, especially during the time that a fragmentation is surfacing. Not all fragmented parts that surface are real fragmented person-parts that belong to the person who is being healed. For this reason, before we embark on any ministry, in Jesus' name we reject divination and bind deception, illusion and delusion, commanding them not to interfere or communicate. We also ask Jesus to ensure the person-part has a safe passage up to the surface as the enemy in some form or other often seeks to hinder this. We ask God to keep the person in His love and peace as they submit to the process and allow their fragmented part to surface. Within the context of ministry to fragmented person-parts, there are two distinct categories of fragmentation that may masquerade as belonging to the person: those that are human intruders and those that are demonic.

Human Spirit Intruders

It is possible for a person to have within them a fragmented person-part that does not belong to them. This is referred to as a human spirit intruder as it belongs to someone else, usually from within the family line. They have part of the person's soul as well as part of their spirit. Such intrusion can only happen where there is some sort of opening that has allowed it, e.g., where a person has already been fragmented or where a foothold has been given in the family generational line. If those who use people for their own evil purposes are unable to get a person to comply with their demands, they may introduce an intruder spirit into that person's body to fulfil their evil purposes, e.g., abuse someone sexually. As we have previously mentioned with regard to captive spirits, satan on occasion may "traffic souls"[32] thus causing confusion, distress and possible destruction. Using human spirit intruders is one way in which he does this.

An intruder spirit person-part can be acquiescent or rebellious, sometimes appearing wicked. We should never make judgements about any intruder but take the time to understand them as so often they are hurting because they have been subjected to some sort of abuse. Any person-part of a gender opposite to that of the person in which they surface is always an intruder. They can torment the person from within or come to the surface and create havoc by behaving in a way that is not in keeping with how the person normally behaves. This is distressing as the person is then accused of actions that they are completely oblivious to and not guilty of as this intruder part within them is not connected to them through the spirit and soul. A person who has a kind heart retains this despite the presence of trauma or of intruder human spirits.

It is important to be aware that many intruders are good at heart, and victims of the circumstances of their birth and family background, used by satan to perpetrate His evil intentions. Many are miserable

---

32 Revelation 18:13 ASV

and fearful and want to be set free from their life of torture and of tormenting others.

Whenever we witnessed a human intruder spirit present in a person, we asked God if He wanted to take them to where they belonged. In doing this, we were careful as to how we expressed it as we did not want the intruder to suffer any further rejection from our words. When the intruder part belonged to someone who was deceased, they were immediately removed.

Whenever the intruder part was not removed then we knew to ask God whether He wanted us to minister healing to them and talk to them about Jesus before they were taken back to where they belonged. This was an amazing privilege for us as we could play a part in bringing this person-part to faith in Christ before they were returned "home". Once the person-part was returned to where they belonged their influence would perhaps encourage that healed and restored person to have faith in Jesus.

Intruder human spirits may surface in a person displaying any one of the different fragmentation forms previously discussed. Some intruder human spirits attach themselves to a fragmented child-part and are like a shadow, always behind that part. This allows them to torment the person-part and, therefore, the adult. The presence of an intruder human spirit is against God's order for creation and contrary to His desire for His people and has the potential for disorder, dissension, breaking up of relationships and disgrace etc.

An intruder human spirit does not know anything about the person within whom they are captive other than what that they have witnessed. When Jesus returns them to where they belong, He ensures that they cannot recall any of this.

Once we are given insight that a fragmentation is an intruder human spirit, we can ask God to send an angel to take that part back to where they belong or, if He wishes, we minister to them in His name. We do not have authority to command intruder human spirits to leave in Jesus' name because they are people and have been given freedom of will. However, God will take them back to where they belong as this aligns with His order of creation.

Although satan's plan is to use intruder human spirits to destroy people, his plan is foiled when they seek healing because many of them come to faith in Jesus. Just as our enemy aims to destroy two people with the one action (the person with the intruder and the intruder) so also ministry in the name of Jesus sets two people free at the one time.

An Example where a Human Spirit Intruder manifested in a Person as a Divided Soul Person-part

Sometimes what appears to be a divided soul in one person can in fact be two person-parts, one belonging to the person themselves and the other to a human spirit intruder. The person can be so used to the thinking that comes from the intruder that they look on it as their own and so are pulled in two directions. This happened to a man who wanted to follow God and serve him.

He was on fire for God when he first became a Christian but since then had succumbed to depression because of serious rejection experienced throughout life. In his early life he had dabbled with the occult and, later, when things became miserable for him through depression, he contacted an occultic source once again. Through ministry God healed this man from depression but there was an interesting development that brought the presence of a human spirit intruder to light.

To his great delight, he wrote a book within a week but when we asked what it was about, we realised that it included material that could well have been damaging to a reader's mental health. He adamantly refused to acknowledge that he had any responsibility towards his readers even though he was a Christian, and declared that he wanted to write the book for his own glory and that he was just writing things as they really were. We didn't agree that it was normal to see frightening pictures in our heads as a consequence of reading a book written by a Christian. His mind-set on the writing of this book was so strongly the antithesis of what he lived out as a person with high morality and expectations of others and a desire to serve God that we were puzzled. He just did not want to change from seeking his own glory nor from following goals that would serve him.

It was at this point that God revealed the cause. The "foreign" thinking was actually coming from a human spirit intruder. A simple prayer asking God to send an angel to remove the intruder and return him to where he belonged set the man free from the apparent contradictory goals. At the following meeting he told us that he was re-writing his book and that it was to be to God's glory.

A strategic form of intruder human spirit is a "familiar" human spirit which can be inherited, remaining at all times within the person, or flitting in and out. When a person has a familiar human intruder spirit, it is so familiar to the person that they don't recognise that anything is wrong. This familiar spirit may even talk to them in a way that makes them think it is Jesus, and so it can be one way that the enemy uses to waylay the Christian and give false information. A familiar spirit slowly eats its way through the will and the mind of the person, taking control; therefore, after removing a familiar spirit, it is essential to cleanse the mind and memories of the person from all the influences and effects, and to pray that their mind and will be strengthened. Frequently they need to be encouraged to practice strengthening their will by making choices. The familiar spirit can use demonic spirits from any of the realms and so spirits of Ahab, Lucifer, Death etc., may also be present.

Marks

A human intruder spirit when removed can leave its mark in a person. The mark is a human spirit imposter, whereas the intruder human spirit is a human spirit infiltrator. A mark is like an outline left by a human spirit intruder (infiltrator) and gives grounds for the human spirit intruder to do as they like as though still in position. The word, "figuratively" can be God's way of revealing that there is not a human spirit intruder but there is a human spirit intruder mark which essentially gives a right for the intruder to return. We can ask Jesus to send an angel to remove it. It is preferable to make sure that, when asking God to send an angel to remove an intruder human spirit, we also ask Him to remove any mark with its influences and effects and any imprints (left by demonic) as well. Then we can ask God to cleanse the person for healing. This may be a process.

Leaving a mark is like leaving a scent and, when left on a person, it acts like a beacon, being a point of contact that gives legal ground for entry to other intruder human spirits. Because an intruder human spirit is responsible for leaving its mark, we have no authority to command it to go in Jesus' name. Instead, we need to ask God to send an angel to remove it.

It can be helpful to the person receiving ministry to understand all that has happened and how healing is taking place, but we must exercise sensitivity and discernment to know when, if at all, to disclose information such as the presence of intruder human spirits. Some people would find this revelation distressing and condemn themselves. We listen to God at all times and follow His leading. There have been times when it was sufficient to pray that God would remove "what does not belong to the person" (in our minds referring to an intruder human spirit). God knows what we are thinking as we pray. The intruder may be a part human spirit of a grandparent or some other relative who has long since died. In some situations, the client may already have a sense of there being something like an intruder human spirit present. It is amazing how God makes many aware spiritually of what is going on within. Being able to express this without being made to feel foolish is often a great relief.

Prayers of protection include asking God to release angels to stop any intruder human spirits from entering a person. When a meeting is about to take place, we can ask God to ensure that, for those attending, only the person He created for the body attends the meeting and that only the part that is normally up on the surface will be present.

Demonic copy

Another form of fragmentation is a demonic copy of a person-part already present. One demon cannot do much to imitate a human being and so it takes several demonic spirits coming together to generate emotions, memory, facial expressions and movements or gestures necessary to form a copy (a counterfeit) of a person-part. This copy can be quite convincing so we have to be alert to the possibility.

When a copy first surfaces, it will look around furtively and take a few seconds to adjust to its surroundings and start imitating the person-part. Because it knows a bit about our ministry, it will engage convincingly in conversation. At this early stage, it can be readily recognised as demonic because it looks "lost" and behaves out of line with our previous experiences of the person-part. With each appearance the copy becomes quicker at adjusting and increasingly deceptive. However, it can be recognised because, either the tiny personal details that we have come to know in the real fragmented person-part are missing, or some characteristics just don't ring true. They literally are copycats but they take the truth and twist it. In one person, who had many fragmented parts, each within the context of ministry having a different name to distinguish them, it had appeared to some of the child-parts that one called Martha had been hurting one called Lydia. What came to light was that the copycat of Martha, and not Martha herself, had been responsible but because this was such a good copy, the other fragmented parts had thought it was actually Martha.

Copies may be present in those who have been through satanic rituals but they occasionally appear in a person who does not like themselves and so seeks attention. Copies may lead to false memory syndrome. We must always be on the alert for a false memory and remember every time a person-part is surfacing to bind spirits of deception, illusion and delusion in Jesus' name and command them not to interfere or communicate. Similarly, we do this for the spirit of divination and remain observant and discerning. God guides us throughout.

In Christ, we take authority over anything demonic so we can pray our usual prayers to command any copycat to leave the person-part in Jesus' name and go to Jesus' feet.

False Video

A "video" having a mix of true and false memories, together with false intruder parts (human spirit intruders and demonic copies) may be placed within a person by satan. It is deception. It will sometimes be present in someone who has been frequently fragmented through witchcraft or satanism and is intended to hinder the person from being fully healed and released. If not recognised as such, it can lead those who are ministering healing to the person on a merry-go-round of fruitless ministry and confusion, thereby causing hopelessness in everyone, especially the person seeking help. The aim of satan would be that those doing ministry would abandon their efforts to help because they had mistakenly come to the conclusion that the victim was just seeking attention.

Our enemy's intention is that ministry counsellors and client alike are discredited and that the person remains unhealed. He may use others, who are looking on with unbelief, to add discouragement to those who are doing their best to help a fragmented person. No-one is ever supposed to recognise the video as such, and, in having it removed, be able to reach the core of the person who truly needs healing.

Only God can show us whether there is a video, in which case He will remove it if we ask Him to do so. We see the heart of love in God the Father who surrounds such a person with those who will follow His leading. I emphasise once more that we must always be on the alert and double check everything with the help of the Holy Spirit.

What the enemy does through a video is disjointed, distorted, exaggerated and in disarray. When we asked God what opening the enemy had used to plant this video within the person, He told us it was because of the person's ancestors who were "barbaric, ruthless, and totally devoid of feelings". In thirty years of this ministry to people, we only came across one in whom a video had been planted. It seems to be extremely rare and there is no need to fear such things as long as we stay close to God's leading. A video is ninety-nine per cent truth, sometimes out of order or sequence, and sometimes including events that actually don't belong to the person. Its purpose is to confuse both the person with the video and those ministering. Some of the child-parts in the video may have memories that are reality for the person and that re-appear within true person-parts once the video has been removed. A cloak of deception may be placed over a person by the enemy to conceal the video. Jesus may choose to leave that in place for a time so as to conceal from the enemy that He is healing the person.

As we come to the end of our discussion on the process of healing a person with fragmented person-parts, a song comes to mind, one sung by Pinocchio[33], which describes well the freedom that those who have been fragmented may experience on release from their captivity,

---

33 I've Got No Strings, Ned Washington, Pinocchio, 1940, Walt Disney

> I've got no strings
> To hold me down
> To make me fret, or make me frown
> I had strings
> But now I'm free
> There are no strings on me
>
> Hi-ho the me-ri-o
> That's the only way to go
> I want the world to know
> Nothing ever worries me
>
> I've got no strings
> So I have fun
> I'm not tied up to anyone
> They've got strings
> But you can see
> There are no strings on me.

I have written the following jingle to help us remember these twelve different forms of fragmentation and some of the ways they affect people.

Fragmentation Song

> A full fragmentation goes into the dark
> Locked away right from the start
> Only brought up when about to be used
> Poor little person, so abused
>
> A partial fragmentation is full of fear
> Only peeps out to see what's there
> Better in the dark and out of sight
> Until it's safe to go into the light

A self-fragmentation says, "No, I'll not!
I don't want to give it a thought
I'll hide away until the day
I can come up and have my own way"

Slumbering spirits, sleepy as can be
Life's too much for them you see
Their spirits grieved, again and again
They opt right out to dull the pain

Semi-fragmentations won't face the facts
They dump their troubles in their little backpacks
Shrug their shoulders through the strife
And says to themselves, "Well, that's just life!"

A divided soul is "two-way Jack"
One going this way, one going that!
Double minded they will be
But their heart is good, you'll see!

A torn soul is ripped apart
Hurt by words or lack of tact
Needs some comfort and some love
From our Father up above

Captive spirits are taken away
To dark, dark dungeons, there to stay
In torment and agony, they will be
Until Lord Jesus sets them free

A personal fragmentation is Jesus' own way
Of saving a child from utter dismay
Done in love, done for their good
Protecting their life as only He could

Intruder spirits don't belong
Placed there to do some wrong
Some have bad hearts, most have good
But struggle with fear until understood

A video is full-on deception
Never is there any exception
Take heed lest you are lured
The Spirit will guide – be assured

SECTION 2

HEART MATTERS

"Behold, You desire truth in the inward parts,
And in the hidden part You will make me to know wisdom."

Psalms 51:6

Chapter 2.1
Healing of the Heart

*"Content with who they are and where they are,
un-anxious, they'll live at peace."*
Zephaniah 3:13b MSG

As we journey through life with the Holy Spirit, those of us who have been seeking God's healing, perhaps using material like that outlined in these books,[34] may have received a good measure of freedom. We may have experienced some aspects of inner healing,[35] restoration of spiritual attributes,[36] deliverance,[37] and integration of healed fragmented person-parts.[38] It can be alarming for us then if subsequently we become aware that our emotions are once again spiralling out of control. Old fears and rejections are surfacing and we blame ourselves for, "losing our healing". We feel as if our world is falling apart and that we don't know who we truly are.

At first, we may be able to maintain our new-found freedom and reliance upon God and the truth of His Word while these intense feelings surface sporadically. However, if the disruptive emotional upheaval increases in duration and intensity, it can be a sign that we have a hurting, broken

---

34 The Ministry of the Father's Heart, Books 1-3
35 Journey of Discovery, chapter 2.4
36 Unveiling our New Identity in Christ, section 1
37 Unveiling our New Identity in Christ, section 2
38 Divine Restoration: Embracing a Life Free from Fear, section 1

heart. When we realise that our misery is coming from an as yet unhealed part of us, fears of having lost our healing and being somehow to blame are put to rest.

In the last section we focussed on healing fragmented soul and spirit person-parts. Now we will direct our attention to healing our broken hearts. A build-up of stress and pressure can lead to swings in mood: alternating between feeling intensely rejected and giving vent to anger, and feeling guilty and miserable over our behaviour towards others. It is a battle between two worlds. Peter Wilson describes such turmoil as "War of the Worlds" in his song, "Some Kind of Love"[39]

> "Blue is the big sky we're rolling towards
> The road underneath us familiar as home
> And we talk about 'War of the Worlds'
> You tell me for years that you've felt so alone
> You'd give up your life to find someone your own
> And we sail on into the sky.
>
> I'm like a creature livin' underground
> I squint at the light
> Pushin' up the dirt with my hands
> trying to get into the light
> I'm tired tonight
> I need to find some kind of love
>
> I'm not a star I'm an ordinary man
> I'm broken and foolish like everyone else
> I'm lookin' for somethin' that's true
> Warm is the sun as it bleaches the sky
> Jesus, I need to feel love to get by
> I need to feel somethin' now
>
> I'm like a creature livin' underground

---

39 The Wonder of the Cross, Robin Mark, Live from Christian Fellowship Church, Belfast, 2003

> I squint at the light
> Pushin' up the dirt with my hands
> Trying to get into the light
> I'm tired tonight
> I need to find some kind of love
>
> I need You…"

These lyrics describe what is happening during this turmoil. A part of our heart, holding extreme emotional overload of perceived rejection and self-rejection, has been pushed out of the way in an effort to cope and has thus become buried. This buried part of the heart is, "pushin' up the dirt with my hands, trying to get into the light" and, "lookin' for somethin' that's true…needing to feel somethin' now." The person is, metaphorically, "pushin' dirt" out of the way through giving vent to their feelings. They are looking for change and for love, "looking for a place in this world."

The good news is that,

> *"The Lord is close to all whose hearts are crushed by pain, and he is always ready to restore the repentant one."* Psalms 34:18 TPT

In this section we will discuss what causes such upheaval in our hearts, how we cope when under stress and how God restores us.

These emotions can be extremely strong and almost overwhelming as they surface, so this is a healing that God usually chooses to do after He has restored and strengthened us in other ways. When I was asking God how He wanted me to write these books, He told me to do so chronologically as that would illustrate His overall direction of healing. He does, however, vary this, choosing the best way for each person.

In healing our hearts, God brings any broken parts of our hearts out of the darkness into the light so that any negative strong emotions and beliefs can be released. Such healing frees us into being totally secure in who we are and so we find our true place in this world. There are two separate processes: restoration of the inner child and the prodigal and restoration of any alter ego and core identity.

Chapter 2.2

The Inner Child and Prodigal and their Restoration

"I praise you because I am fearfully and wonderfully made; your works are wonderful; I know that full well."
Psalms 139:14

"Finding our place in this world."

Inner Child

Many of us have experienced a form of sudden freedom at a later time in life when we throw off the shackles of what is expected of us, and allow ourselves to enter the world of a child once again with gay abandon. How many of us have found delight in joining in with our grandchildren's fun and imaginative games?

What about those whose ability to do this is locked away?

Everyone has an inner child: the part of the person that is fun-loving, transparent, and trusting, retaining childlikeness (not childishness). God intends that we retain this childlikeness as an aspect of our total nature as we age. Jesus told His listeners that being as a child, full of trust, was necessary to enter His kingdom,

> *"And he said: "Truly I tell you, unless you change and become like little children, you will never enter the kingdom of heaven."* Matthew 18:3

If at any stage in life this part of us perceives itself as not good enough, not accepted, or in some way needing to change it can opt out in deep despair, becoming buried.

We can witness the potential for growing loss of childlikeness in children as they are growing up. At age three they may draw and recite rhymes with unhesitating enthusiasm. At age five, they may still perceive their "performances" as pleasing to everyone. By age nine they are comparing their efforts with those of others and by eleven they are beginning to learn that their best is sometimes judged as not *the* best and so their enthusiasm and spontaneity can be curbed. As adults we have learned to put away childish things and rightly so, but all too often we have learned to put away childlike things, the good characteristics of a child such as trust, innocence, the sense of belonging and self-acceptance.

There are many possible contributing factors that can cause an inner child to become buried: constant criticism; never being listened to; living in fear of doing wrong. When subjected to consistent negativity, a child may feel that they need to become what others expect of them and so "shut down" their identity in an effort to please. Any reactive feelings of anger or injustice may be suppressed out of fear of further rejection or punishment and lead to their inner child being buried. As they grow up, they struggle with the "two much and too many" in life.

This loss of childlikeness can happen through circumstances, through being assessed and through misperceptions. Parents, guardians and teachers may not be aware of any negative effect they are having on a child and could be upset to think that their words were being interpreted by the child as indicating that they were "not good enough" or "not wanted". A child's mind observes and processes things literally and so offhand comments can have deep significance, for example, "grow up", "you're no daughter of mine", or "you're good for nothing". Some families believe that they are doing what is best for a child by forcing them to suppress emotion, as in the command, "don't be a cry-baby". Any negative emotions can become exaggerated in a child's mind, and reinforced by the enemy, and the child can become confused. Happily, many children are nurtured within an ethos of unconditional love and can understand that they are loved even when they have done wrong, and so grow up feeling secure in who they are.

The child who struggles becomes governed by fear and will try to be accepted by doing what is expected. They learn to believe that acceptance depends on what they do rather than on who they are. It's worth us all pausing here and reflecting on how much we take our identity from what we do, sometimes to the extent that we avoid dealing with inner stresses. In some very real sense this fearful, hurting child can hold the adult captive.

When a child consistently experiences a pattern of perceived rejection in early life, the person may grow up with a fear of rejection. In trying to avoid feeling rejected, they may keep at a distance from people and accuse others of being unfriendly. It is as though they have placed an invisible barrier between themselves and others. They believe that there is something wrong with them and dislike themselves, continuing to reject who they really are and going on a downward spiral. This can have consequences on two aspects of the person's life; on the inner child of the person and on the person as they are growing up. The inner child may lose sense of their true identity and be buried. The part left growing up may reach the point where too much emotional upheaval causes overload and, unintentionally, they create one or more alter egos to hold some of the pain (see chapter 2.3). In this way their hearts become divided and they lose sight of who they really are at the core of their being.

As adults, we learn to adjust to our perceived inadequacies in various ways but now and again the internal struggle comes to the fore. On the one hand we hear the gentle voice of the Spirit of God encouraging and affirming us and on the other we hear our own voice bringing self-condemnation and self-rejection. On the one hand is the truth of God, that each one of us is loved, valued, worthwhile and has a place that is unique in this world while, on the other hand, is the negative thinking, the mindset and feelings that we have developed through our interpretation of life. We hear words and sense attitudes through the lens of self-rejection and continue to feel unworthy and of no use. We may lose spontaneity, blame ourselves when things go wrong and believe that we don't matter. The question arises, "how can such deeply hurting people move beyond their self-rejection, their pre-occupation with their own inadequacy, their feelings of homelessness, into finding their place in this world?"

Anything that happens to the person happens to each part of the person and so inner trauma has an emotional effect on the heart of an inner child as well as on the heart of the part maturing into adulthood. Some damage may probably be done during childhood, but may well continue into adulthood because of learned ways of dealing with further stress and pressure. Both the inner child and the adult use self-preserving measures when they feel unable to cope in life.

Since the inner child has been separated from their true identity and is "lost", it is as though they wander away from "home" and search until they find a place where they belong. The remaining part of the person that matures into adulthood also has an identity which, through ongoing stress and pressure, may also become buried (chapter 2.3). Since, in each person who came for ministry, God chose to heal the heart of the inner child prior to healing that of the adult, I will describe the healings in that order.

Although, so far, I have described everything as a consequence of inner turmoil and perceived rejection or stress and pressure, the driving force behind such inner separation in the heart is demonic. Evil spirits ride in on emotional upheaval and see it as an opportunity to influence and reinforce a person's negative thinking about themselves. Their aim is to steal, kill and destroy[40].

Where a person has little or no concept of how evil spirits can influence their thinking and consequent behaviour, they can believe that every thought is theirs and so have two contradictory streams of thoughts, each completely divorced from the another. This causes mental confusion and an inability to think straight. The pressure in their heads can build up to an unbearable pitch so that they want to end it all. Reasoning with such negativity isn't effective if demonic is present because it cannot be reasoned with. Only God can break through the destructive deception. When a person comes to Him for help, He guides them to freedom step by step.

Examples

After receiving progressive healing, and living in her newfound freedom for some time, one person began to find herself increasingly going down into a pit of despair. Everywhere she went she believed that people were rejecting her, that nobody liked her and that nothing had changed from when she had been a child. She accused me of rejecting and ignoring her and became obsessively pre-occupied with the idea that she wanted me to be her best friend. Repeatedly, I responded patiently to the verbal attacks but all to no avail. For weeks the accusations were directed at me. I knew her well and was confident that this was not in character but couldn't find a way to help her break through. I determined that she was not going to make me a prisoner and had to be careful not to react to the injustice aimed at me, but rather to choose the path of patient love and encouragement. Light began to break through once God revealed that one of the spirits affecting her was a Jezebel spirit. This spirit had come in on the rejection and jealousy that the person had felt as a child, and was now continuing to reinforce and drive this thinking, thus making her feel unwanted and isolated. Eventually it had become "too much

---

40 John 10:10

and too many" for her and, in rejecting her inner child, this aspect of her had given up on life and become buried with her emotional pain.

Although no longer actively participating in her life, the inner child deep within continued to influence her thinking and emotions. When she had initially come for ministry, she had received Jesus as her Saviour and her Lord and, thereafter, had benefitted through much healing from hurt and brokenness, including restoration and intermingling of fragmented child-parts. This healing had greatly helped the adult and she had thought her need of ministry was over. She had been relatively free from her former mindset for most of the time since. When, in desperation, she called for help, she was no longer able to fight the very strong thoughts and feelings of rejection and jealousy. She had blamed herself for slipping back into the old ways and had struggled on for some weeks, but was becoming more and more desperate and talked of wanting to opt out of life. As we prayed together God gave us insight that this fresh upheaval was coming from her inner child, who was surfacing with the full intensity of the emotions and beliefs with which she had been buried.

For many, this experience is extremely frightening, especially for those who have felt very close to God and alive spiritually and who, suddenly, experience a spiritual deadness. This deadness in their spirit affects their desire and ability to worship God and to deepen their relationship with Him. They may feel that they don't want to go to church, read the Bible or pray, and yet at the same time are puzzled because those were the very things that were so important to them.

Once a person seeks help from God and is willing to allow this buried part to participate in their life again, He will release their inner child. The inner child may come right up to the surface for ministry in which case the adult will be behind the scenes, as it were, looking on but not participating in any conversation. Alternatively, they may come sufficiently near to the surface to make their memories and emotions felt in the person themselves in which case ministry continues with this person on behalf of their inner child. Restoration can take place in either scenario but is much easier when talking face to face with the inner child.

When an inner child surfaces, they do so with intense feelings of rejection, hatred, and anger and may vent their wrath on those around them. For some, their rejection has been so deep that they refer to themselves by names such as "nothing" or "nobody". These feelings of not being wanted are dogmatically held to as truth, and so influence them to such a degree that they are unable to acknowledge God's truth. They may believe that the bad things that happened in their life demonstrated how unacceptable they were as a person and hold that as truth. It is absolutely essential that any person ministering healing to such a hurting damaged person demonstrate unconditional, long-suffering love and acceptance while at the same time affirming what is truth.

The conflict is one of light versus darkness, of God's kingdom versus satan's dominion. The latter seeks to divide and conquer. God seeks to bring everyone into unity within themselves and between themselves and others. He reveals truth and restores internal harmony, security and significance. The enemy deceives and exaggerates, destroying people and relationships. He, the enemy, focuses on influencing a person's thoughts, labelling facts as truth.

This battle in the mind between what is fact and therefore perceived as truth, and what is *the* truth according to God's word, ended for this person when we made the distinction between what had been fact but was not *the* truth, and what was *the* truth according to who she is in Christ. Once this key was discerned, she made a choice to believe *the* truth that was revealed through God's word rather than the truth that had been fact in her life.

In another, the facts were that others had walked over her all her life, had not listened to her but had talked over her when she was speaking, and had never considered what she would like, nor given her choices.

This had been interpreted into a truth that she was second best, only good at doing what she was told to do, and that her views and ideas were useless and unimportant. This thinking was reinforced into adulthood and, even though she knew *the* truth according to God's word, she was unable to shake the wrong self-perception of her truth until her inner child and, later on her alter ego, were each healed and restored. Throughout life, she had exercised very strong self-control because of fear of disapproval, but rather than being a fruit of the Spirit, it was the fruit of self-preservation and had to be renounced. It had held her in a form of captivity, in contrast to the freedom that comes with self-control that grows through the grace of God.

Yet another person thought that she was a waste of time simply because she bought a pair of shoes that didn't fit her.

Until the person can grasp the lie and move from being governed by feelings, to making choices based on *the* truth, they cannot move forward into freedom. Because of the internal battle they can feel very tired and as though their head is about to explode. The battle is fierce, but the path of healing is gentle and one of perseverance. Once light breaks through, and the person makes a choice to believe the truth about what God says despite their experiences past and present, they are on the road to breakthrough. They need to maintain their stand on the truth in the face of ongoing internal opposition, in which case it is then straightforward in Jesus' name to command the spirits of rejection, hatred and anger, and any other evil spirit such as Jezebel to leave. Once the spirits have left, it becomes easier for the person to maintain their freedom in resisting wrong perceptions. If anyone reading this is being troubled in this way, please take time to ask Jesus to shine His light into the darkness and show you what has happened. The Psalmist writes,

> *"If I say, 'Surely the darkness will hide me and the light become night around me,' even the darkness will not be dark to you; the night will shine like the day, for darkness is as light to you."* Psalms 139:11-12

As God leads, you can choose to reject any negative beliefs about yourself and embrace the truth that God reveals, that you are totally loved. Robin Mark[41] expresses this cry from deep within us with the following words,

> I hear You're in the business of healing hearts
> That's why I've come
> But I don't even know where I should start
> I've seen so many places, cried a million tears
> But nothing ever met my need
> And no-one ever calmed my fear
>
> And only You can reach me there
> Only You can heal
> My prayer is that by Your Spirit
> You might reveal
> The part of my heart that you need to heal
> The part of my heart that you need to heal
>
> Well, the heart is deceitful above all, Sir
> So said your servant
> Has he ever said a truer word
> I've found so many secrets locked inside of me
> And only You can make them known
> For only You possess the key

When we are spiritually strong and alert and able to release the truth into our damaged inner child, we will walk further towards freedom. God restores the inner child carefully, opening doors of pain one by one so that the person does not become overwhelmed, even though at times it can seem unbearable. Each time the child is faced with a truth that opposes their thinking, there follows a time of exploring it to test it. Once they receive that truth they don't waver.

---

41 Part of My Heart, Robin Mark, Days of Elijah, Novatech Studio, Belfast 1995

The Prodigal

Because rejection, and specifically Jezebel, has been at work all along reinforcing the perceived rejection within the inner child, the "too much and too many" not only lead to the inner child opting out of life but also to self-rejection within that child. This rejection of self, fed by Jezebel, with thoughts of feeling unworthy, no good, and about to be replaced with someone who is better in some way, can become rejection of who they are at the core of their being and so a part of them holding that identity and the potential for security in that identity is rejected and pushed away. This part of the inner child (the prodigal) feels lost and wanders looking for their home and asking the question, "Is there a vision I can call my own?"

In a similar way to the inner child, even when not actively participating in life, the buried prodigal influences the person's thoughts, feelings and actions at a conscious level with a feeling that they never belong. Their feelings of misery, consistent apprehension, loss of expectation, fear of making wrong decisions, and weighing up the consequences of actions so as to avoid trouble, may filter up to the adult-part at the surface. Just as the prodigal in scripture returned home smelling of pigs, so also the prodigal on returning to life is influenced by demonic spirits and accompanied by insecurities. As God restores the prodigal there is a cry from within for some kind of love, a love that knows *me* as *me* and loves *me*. Along with this is the cry to belong and wanting to find *my* place in this world. The words of this song[42] portray such searching,

> The wind is moving
> But I am standing still
> A life of pages
> Waiting to be filled
> A heart that's hopeful

---

[42] Place in This World, Michael W. Smith / Amy Grant / Wayne Kirkpatrick, Sony/ATV Music Publishing LLC, Universal Music Publishing Group, Capitol Christian Music Group, Music Services, Inc

> A head that's full of dreams
> But this becoming
> Is harder than it seems
> Feels like I'm
>
> Looking for a reason
> Roaming through the night to find
> My place in this world
> My place in this world
> Not a lot to lean on
> I need Your light to help me find
> My place in this world
> My place in this world
>
> If there are millions
> Down on their knees
> Among the many
> Can you still hear me?
> Hear me asking
> Where do I belong?
> Is there a vision
> That I can call my own?
> Show me I'm
>
> Looking for a reason
> Roaming through the night to find
> My place in this world……

This healing can feel like a long, very, very narrow bridge over turbulent water. In rejecting who they are, the inner child rejects the identity that God has given them. Since the enemy is prowling around looking for whom he may devour (1 Peter 5:8) he sees this as an opportunity in which to introduce a false identity, often through using a Lucifer spirit. He uses his strategies against the prodigal to crush the whole person. I pause here to reinforce something really important. Evil spirits are merely opportunists and use tools of deception and thievery to accomplish their desires. They have no right to interfere with a child of God but will do so, if allowed, until evicted. Our goal in Jesus' name is to have them evicted.

Since the person with a lost identity is easily moved to jealousy of others (aided and abetted by a spirit of Jezebel) such jealousy must be repented of, i.e., turned away from, before deliverance can take place. The person also needs to turn from rejecting themselves in their attempts to please others. No matter what has happened or what has been said in the past, whether intentional or unintentional, before anything happens Jesus has already promised to rescue us.[43] God has His hand on the prodigals and declares, "they are mine".

In my experience, a prodigal part has sometimes been divided in two, one part passionate about knowing Jesus and the other opposing His kingdom because they've been indoctrinated into believing that Lucifer is good, and Jesus is bad. This split within the prodigal is caused by the Lucifer spirit who wants to rule in the person's life, giving them a new but false identity. He does this by feeding in lies and deceiving with his actions but, because God has created us in love, we all have a knowledge of Him deep within, and so any action on Lucifer's part to draw us away from that truth cannot fully succeed. Because God created us for relationship with Him, He has ensured that there will always be the potential for restoration to what He intended for us.

Ministry to this part that has believed lies is, to say the very least, interesting. Try and convince someone who really believes that black is white and white is black that the opposite is true. It's not easy. Some examples of this come to mind from ministry.

---

43 2 Thessalonians 3:3

Examples

In one example, the first part of the prodigal had come and listened attentively to all that I had said about Jesus, as she journeyed through the process of being released from emotional hurt and the associated demonic. There came a day when, out of the blue, she told me that words were coming to her and she began to sing, "I've got the joy, joy, joy deep down in my heart"[44]. I was jubilant because, unknown to this prodigal part, joy had been missing from the adult until she had been healed, at which point this very same song had risen up from her spirit. I took this as a cue and explained that Jesus was the One who was giving her joy in her heart and would she like to ask Him to help her. This she readily agreed to.

The story was different with the second prodigal part. She first appeared when I was on the beach with the first prodigal part building sandcastles. She surfaced, replacing the first prodigal part, and got to work on the sand digging a hole and informing me that she was making a cauldron and went on to talk about making spells. When I queried this, she told me that they were good spells. We had quite a discussion! How exciting it was when, as we were walking back to the car, she told me that words were coming to her, "I've got the joy, joy, joy deep down in my heart".[45] Again, I took this as a cue to helping her receive Jesus in her heart. After this she found it relatively easy to adapt to a new way of thinking, based on the truth of God's love. It seemed that Jesus was using this song to reveal Himself to each part of this particular person. I am glad to say that the inner child and prodigal part of this person have been totally healed and brought together, and are now vivacious in their joy in Jesus.

This dichotomy occurred in another person; their first part readily received the truth about Jesus and responded to His love, whereas their second part had been heavily indoctrinated into believing that Lucifer was good and Jesus bad. Everything that we as Christians

---

44   I've got Joy, Joy, Joy Deep in my Heart, George William Cooke, 1884-1951
45   I've got Joy, Joy, Joy Deep in my Heart, George William Cooke, 1884-1951

know to be true of Jesus had been credited to Lucifer and everything bad blamed on Jesus. No matter how often or in how many different ways I talked about Jesus and how He had helped me, they seemed unable to receive the truth. Their mindset of false premises and beliefs was well established.

Eventually I gave up and, in desperation, suggested she ask Jesus to show her the truth about Himself. Within seconds He had shown her two scenarios in the spirit and given her freedom to study them and come to her own conclusion. To the left and in front of her she saw a group of people who represented those whom she knew and had obeyed. To the right and in front she saw a figure whom she somehow knew was Jesus. The people on the left were smiling and holding out gifts and sweets to her. Jesus wasn't smiling and wasn't holding anything out to her. His arms hung at His sides with His hands held out. When asked about how He looked she said that He looked sad - sad for her. She looked again at the group to the left and now saw that although they were smiling on their faces, they "weren't smiling inside". She looked again at Jesus and saw that He felt as He looked. He wanted her to go to Him of her own accord. The group also wanted her. She looked first at one then at the other repeatedly. After some thought she chose to go to Jesus. As soon as she started to go towards Him, He came to her holding out His arms to put them around her. She held out her hand and He took it and told her that He would walk with her. I stood beside her marvelling at how easy it had been for Jesus to bring light into her darkness.

Both of these prodigal parts responded to the loving acceptance of Jesus. An unconditional loving acceptance without demands turned out to be what they had been searching for.

As I have said before, child-parts have an amazing ability to see and hear Jesus and it is the same for the inner child. I believe this is because, when after they surface and are released from distress, their focus is easily placed on Jesus without any distraction. This inspires me to believe that the same can be true for us as adults in an adult world if we put our distractions to the side and focus on Jesus, listening for what He wants to tell us.

Another person who had come for ministry had three parts to her prodigal, each distinct in their outlook and behaviour. One was focused on her mummy, one repeatedly told me, "I only go where Jesus goes", and one loved to have fun and play games.

When Jesus was healing my prodigal child, I sensed that He was stripping away the false fleshly ways that I had used when trying to cope with rejection. Words of a song[46] rose up from my spirit confirming what I had heard,

> "When the music fades
> All is stripped away
> And I simply come
> Longing just to bring
> Something that's of worth
> That will bless your heart
>
> I'll bring you more than a song
> For a song in itself
> Is not what you have required
> You search much deeper within
> Through the way things appear
> You're looking into my heart"

All the prodigals are attacked in their minds and have a battle between two types of self-control, one that is the fruit of the Spirit and the other the fruit of determination without the grace of God. Strong's Exhaustive Concordance defines grace as "especially the divine influence upon the heart and its reflection in life; including gratitude." This song[47] comes to mind,

---

46 The Heart of Worship, Matt Redman and Andy Piercy, Intimacy 1998
47 Album: Living Waters, Jimmy Swaggart 1985

> Let your living waters flow over my soul
> Let your Holy Spirit come and take control
> Of every situation that has troubled my mind
> All my cares and burdens on to You I roll
>
> Jesus, Jesus, Jesus
> Father, Father, Father
> Spirit, Spirit, Spirit
>
> Come now Holy Spirit, and take control
> Hold me in Your loving arms and make me whole,
> Wipe away all doubt and fear and take my pride
> Draw me to Your love and keep me by Your side.

All prodigals have had a veil put over their minds by the enemy so as to hinder their being able to see Jesus. This veil needs to be removed in Jesus' name. Sometimes when they find it difficult to talk about what has happened to them, they might act it out as having happened to a doll or a soft toy. On other occasions they use them to illustrate what is happening at the time. One prodigal part put a cover over her doll to hide her from view and then removed it. She was showing me that there was another prodigal part hidden from view and about to come to the surface. Both prodigal parts in a person have good hearts. They are just controlled in different ways by the enemy to reinforce disunity. As we respond with gentleness to any aggression, any antagonism gradually lessens, and the real heart of the child is seen. They don't want to hurt others but are afraid of disobeying the enemy because of the consequences.

As healing comes to its end the prodigal parts are allowed up to the surface occasionally to observe the person's life. Not only have the person and their activities changed but the world has also. For some, mobile phones and ownership of cars seemed strange. One child aged twelve thought she could drive after she had watched me do so. Such is the optimistic confidence of the inner child.

Where there are two or more prodigal parts in a person, once healing in each has been completed, they are asked whether they would be happy to be intermingled back together by Jesus. Sometimes they need to be encouraged to believe that the other one wants them and that they themselves would bring something good to the union. Once this union takes place the prodigal can then be invited to consider joining with the inner child. This is a big step as the prodigal knows that, at one time, they were rejected by the inner child and so they need reassurance that the inner child wants them back. Conversations with the inner child and with the prodigal pave the way towards restoration until, finally, both agree to being intermingled together as one, by Jesus, never to be parted again. Once restored to their rightful place they continue throughout life contributing childlike qualities to the person.

The passage about the dry bones in Ezekiel is a message of hope to a despondent people. Having been exiled in Babylon for ten years the people of Israel had given up hope of the kingdom of Israel ever being revived. They were away from home and didn't belong. The bones, like the people, were dry, having no life in them, and it would take a miracle of God for life to be restored. God speaks into the situation through His prophet,

> *"Dry Bones, Listen to the Message of God."* Ezekiel 37:4

In reading through this passage, we note that Ezekiel prophesied four stages that would bring the dry bones to life,

> *"I'll attach sinews to you and put meat on your bones, cover you with skin and breathe life into you."* Ezekiel 37:6

We can use these four stages to understand four aspects of life-giving healing in the prodigal. Four is the number for completeness.

"I'll attach sinews to you"

The purpose of the sinews, which is a band of tough tissue that attaches a muscle to a bone or some other part, is to enable strength. In this war against self-rejection and fear, which is so often caused by deception, we need strength and that strength is given through the truth and by the grace of God and is resident in our spirits. Receiving God's truth inwardly as to who we are and where we belong changes us from being weak to being strong. Being girded with truth is a source of strength against perceived rejection. We can ask Jesus to remove the influence of deception and help us to see this truth in the midst of our turbulent emotions. So, a first key is to live by the truth.

"(I'll) put meat on your bone"

Another key to rejecting the negativity that has developed in the prodigal part of us is to soak ourselves in God's Word and become transformed by the renewing of our mind rather than being conformed to the world. Our minds are renewed as we think about,

> *"whatsoever things are true, whatsoever things are noble, whatsoever things are just, whatsoever things are pure, whatsoever things are lovely, whatsoever things are of good report-anything that is a virtue or is praiseworthy."* Philippians 4:8

As we fellowship with Jesus, we receive the mind of Christ. Jesus said,

> *"I am the Bread of life."* John 6:35

As we feed on Him, we are nourished and, in the words of Ezekiel, "meat is put on our bones". This second key is relationship with Jesus, the Living Word, through His Spirit.

"(I'll) cover you with skin"

Skin is the outer covering, the protection for the internal organs etc. A third key is to trust in our Heavenly Father to protect us and keep us safe. This means that we stop using defence mechanisms and walk, holding His hand, trusting Him and believing truth. This is frightening for those who have tried to be in control of themselves. We can call out in desperation from the intensity of our fears, "Father me"[48],

> Father, father me, I need your love, I need your love
> Father, father me
> I feel so alone, longing for a home
>
> I need comfort, I need shelter
> I need healing for my soul
> Take this fear that I surrender
> Take me in, take me home, father me
> Father, father me, call me by name, call me by name
> Father, oh please father me, take me to your home
> Adopt me as your own
> I need comfort, I need shelter
> I need healing for my soul
> Take this pain that I surrender
> Take me in, take me home
> Father, father me, I need your love, I need your love
> Father, father me, take me to your home
> Adopt me as your own, father me
> Father me.

The love of our Father God reassures, comforts and heals in many ways. He will take us by the hand through our difficulties. We read in the Gospels of Jesus being in two different storms. In the one He commanded the waves to be still. In the other He invited Peter to walk with Him. Either God will change our difficult circumstances, or He will walk with

---

48 Father Me, Brian Doerksen, Father's House, 1995

us through them. Instead of relying on our self-protections we can lean on our heavenly Father as we learn to face things with courage,

> *"Be strong and very courageous for the Lord your God is with you."*
> Deuteronomy 31:6

When we take our Father's hand, He protects us and strengthens us to face situations. This is like the skin in Ezekiel's prophecy, the covering that protects. Remember that, when Hagar ran away from Sarah because she had dealt harshly with her, the angel of the Lord found her by a spring in the wilderness and asked her,

> *"where have you come from and where are you going?"* Genesis 16: 8

God didn't need to be told because He knew but He was encouraging Hagar to pour out her heart to Him. Our Father wants us to tell Him everything. He wants us to examine what has hurt us or offended us in the light of truth, to acknowledge sin for what it is, and in the light of facing the truth, to forgive and release the pain to Him.

Healing takes place as we move from the bondage of self-control with wrong motive (which may be there to protect self out of fear of retribution or rejection) into self-control that is free and born out of love and that is a fruit of the spirit. When God was healing and restoring my prodigal. He told me to stop trying to work out how people might react and choosing paths that I thought might avoid negative reactions. I was to stop trying to see ahead and, instead, place my hand in God's and trust Him to tell me what I needed to know. It is in living in the love of our Father God that we can reject self-rejection and fear: a love demonstrated by Jesus when He chose to take upon Himself the judgement for our sin so that we could be forgiven, freed from guilt and fear and restored into loving relationship with God.

"(I'll) breathe new life into you"

A fourth key is to ask God to breathe His life into us. As we keep asking God to breathe His life through us, within us, about us, life will be restored to the prodigal part of us. The crushed spirit will be freed, and spirit to Spirit relationship restored. The prodigal part of us will be brought to life with a capital "L". We will find a deeper closeness to our Father, a more profound understanding of the sacrifice of Jesus, a living sense of a Holy God. We will be freed to walk with Him, to talk with Him and to have deep companionship with Him leading us into worshipping Him unceasingly.

In summary the four keys to restoration of the inner child and prodigal are; reject self-rejection and believe the truth that we are loved, fellowship with Jesus in His word and transform our minds, trust in Father God to keep us safe, and continuously receive the life of God through His Spirit.

Finally, God prophesies through Ezekiel,

> *"Therefore, prophesy and say to them: 'This is what the Sovereign Lord says: My people, I am going to open your graves and bring you up from them; I will bring you back to the land of Israel. I will put my Spirit in you and you will live, and I will settle you in your own land. Then you will know that I the Lord have spoken, and I have done it, declares the Lord.'"* Ezekiel 37:12,14

When the healing is complete each of us will experience, deep within our spirits and hearts, an acceptance of ourselves, a confidence that, "I am who I am, I am worthwhile, and I have a place in this world". We will experience greater freedom and security. We will each be able to dream dreams and receive a vision of our own from God. He wants us to be free from all that hinders or slows us down in His Kingdom and to know to the core of our being that He truly loves us. When we believe this truth then we will remain in contentment whenever our emotions waver or our minds are assaulted. God wants us to feel loved and to believe that we are significant and secure, "at home". He says,

> *"I have loved you with an everlasting love and am constant in my affection for you."* Jeremiah 31:3

and Paul affirms,

> *"For we are God's workmanship, created in Christ Jesus to do good works, which God prepared in advance for us to do."* Ephesians 2:10

Once we are healed deep within our hearts from the roots of insecurity and rejection, we move more readily in freedom and joy, not withdrawing, not pushing ourselves to the forefront. We know who we are and what our place in this world is. We are fully content in our identity as a child of God,

> *"whom the Son sets free is free indeed."* John 8:36

The lyrics of a song by Hillsong Worship[49] describe this process of complete healing and restoration of the inner child in finding their identity and their place in this world,

> Who am I that the highest King
> Would welcome me?
> I was lost but He brought me in
> Oh His love for me
> Oh His love for me
>
> Who the Son sets free
> Oh is free indeed
> I'm a child of God, Yes, I am.

---

49   Who You Say I Am, There is More, Hillsong Worship, 2018

Free at last, He has ransomed me
His grace runs deep
While I was a slave to sin
Jesus died for me
Yes, He died for me

Who the Son sets free
Oh, is free indeed.

I'm a child of God, Yes, I am.

In my Father's house
There's a place for me
I'm a child of God
Yes, I am.

I am chosen
Not forsaken
I am who You say I am
You are for me
Not against me
I am who You say I am

I am chosen
Not forsaken
I am who You say I am
You are for me
Not against me.

What can we hope for?

Let's imagine what it would be like in our fellowships if we each believed we were loved, and felt secure and significant. They would be totally safe places in which we could make mistakes and try out things without fear of rejection. In such places we would not be afraid to try doing what we long to do, we would not be afraid of being belittled, we would not fear humiliation and we would thrive in the loving acceptance and encouragement of one another, thus developing in fruitfulness in the ministry to which God has called us. God, through healing and restoring us to confidence in who we are in Christ, restores to us trust, truth, friendship, youth, fun, music, freedom, belonging, confidence, faith, innocence. The list of blessing never ends.

In Jesus Christ we are the most amazing people. In Jesus Christ we can do anything He asks us to do and in Jesus Christ we have the potential to change this nation for the better. In Jesus Christ there is no limit to our ability, to the power of Jesus, to the love of Jesus. There are abilities to teach children in Africa, to lead worship in Bangor, to invite a person to Christ in the Caribbean, to demonstrate the power of the cross in the streets of Belfast. Let's stop rejecting ourselves and begin accepting who we are. Let's stop protecting ourselves by hiding and, instead, allow God to work through us. Let's help and build up one another so that each of us is secure and confident and released to do what in our hearts we long to do. Let's do it and have fun while we do!

Chpater 2.3
The Alter Ego and Core Identity and their Restoration

> *"I will give you the treasures of darkness*
> *and hidden riches of secret places,*
> *That you may know that I, the Lord,*
> *who call you by your name, am the God of Israel."*
> Isaiah 45:3

Alter Ego

If, throughout life, we have increasingly struggled to cope with a range of emotions and repetitively felt over-pressured, we may resort to dumping the excess of emotion on a part of our heart which is then "ignored" and buried. This buried part holding extreme emotional upheaval is called an alter ego. It is not the same as fragmentation. This is a heart issue whereas what we call fragmentation is an issue concerning soul and spirit. Some alter egos may have been denied the opportunity to discover the goodness of God in life because they have been kept solely as dumping grounds for pain and hurt.

We create alter egos in order to cope in life or because we believe that certain emotions are socially unacceptable. We may be trying to project that life for us is good and normal and are often too frightened to admit that anything is wrong. The emotional upheaval from surfacing alter egos has the potential to overwhelm a person, so they must be emotionally stable, living in reality, and spiritually strong before any alter ego is surfaced. Jesus ensures this. He is the only one who can enter our broken hearts and restore them with His love.

Perhaps you have heard the term, "alter ego" associated with the evil side of our nature but such a description does not give an accurate picture. This part of our heart, that has been suppressed, is full of pain with its associated emotions of rejection, fear, anger, and revenge, and as it surfaces, is out of kilter with what the person believes or how they want to behave. This causes great distress to the person because they find it difficult to control, and feel guilty and ashamed of the sudden outbursts and antagonistic feelings that seem out of character.

The truth is that the alter ego is not inherently bad, but because of hurt and perceived abandonment, it is reacting in undesirable ways. The person can be shocked at the venom that comes out from their own mouth and find it very difficult to accept this part of their heart because it is associated with pain and is miserable, tearful, full of regrets, and often angry and vindictive. Issues of shame and guilt appear, therefore understanding and affirmation is needed to reassure the person that they are not evil but are reacting from having been badly hurt or overpressured. They need reassurance, love and healing.

When one person thus affected was offered a doll named after her she found it almost impossible to take it. Somewhere within, she saw the doll as representing who she was at the core of her heart, a part of her heart holding overwhelming emotions that she had rejected and didn't want to know. Over time, as she experienced consistent and accepting love from us, she was able to receive the doll and hold it. This showed us that she was now accepting this part of her that she had pushed away.

Not only does the person initially reject their alter ego but their alter ego also rejects them. The alter ego sees them as "the dumper", and has a real issue with having being "used". Alter egos are troubled and very serious, having strong negative mindsets resistant to change. Gradually, as they embrace new mindsets based on the truth, they let go their previous negative ones together with any associated demonic. As they begin to feel accepted and experience joy, forgiveness towards "the dumper" gradually develops.

Alter egos do not need to progress in age, as do fragmented person parts before they are intermingled. After the alter ego has been released from distress and is free, and is aligning with and enjoying the lifestyle of the adult, they will gradually become united.

Some people may have two or more alter egos, each successive one being created by the previous. Thus, the first alter ego may hold emotions like rejection and, on becoming overloaded, form a second in which to dump the more extreme or socially unacceptable emotions e.g., anger, hatred and a desire to kill. This second alter ego is then held under control by the first.

There can be some sort of veil that hides the second alter ego and which needs removing before it can appear. This veil may be some demonic spirit or a "figment of the imagination" (Jesus' words), i.e., some thought hindrance from within the person themselves. In one person the first alter ego, like the person, had an imaginary world where everything was as they would like it to be. The person had an unreal expectation of others. This "figment of imagination" had veiled the second alter ego. It was only after they recognised that their imaginary world was not a true world in which others lived that they were able to discard it and it was then that the second alter ego surfaced.

Whereas the first alter ego may exhibit strong feelings of rejection and timidity, and along with this, lack of trust and ability to believe that they are loved and accepted, the second alter ego often lashes out in rage and hatred as they surface, protecting themselves in a very different way from what are similar insecurities. In their anger and hatred, they can on occasion come up shouting and screaming and with fists clenched. They can be so unhappy and afraid that they want to kill themselves.

The first alter ego works hard to keep the second one down so as to avoid trouble, and so cannot rest and becomes extremely tired. When this second alter ego is recalling their memories and emotions in the process of healing, the first alter ego may become traumatized afresh and so everything may need to be talked through with this part once again and further trauma released. Life can be extremely fraught during such healing so we must learn to live with our eyes upon Jesus as we work through the difficulties. The person may get impatient wanting healing to be completed more quickly but emotional healing takes time as mindsets need to change. God wants to teach us in the process so that we can remain free, not repeating our mistakes. As we learn, so we can help others.

Some Other Reasons why an Alter Ego is created

An alter ego can be formed through the action of an antichrist spirit that has been passed on generationally as the result of some heresy in the past. The goal of the spirit in creating an alter ego is that the person self-destruct.

This is accomplished through putting a seed of destruction (destructive spirit) in the person's mind or using a spirit like Ahab to plant destructive thoughts. Spirits of antichrist and destruction, working together, can multiply any confusion already in the person's mind making it difficult for them to find the path to freedom. A trusted person standing alongside and ministering to the person helps them to persevere through the storm.

The spirit of Jezebel is yet another spirit aiming at destruction, only this destruction is associated with the calling that God has placed upon the person's life. During one ministry to a person whom we will call Tina (not her real name) from whom the spirit of Jezebel was being evicted, this spirit kept maintaining that it was not Jezebel but Tina. It just would not leave but mimicked being hurt at the idea that I would send it away. I was confident that it was in fact Jezebel because she had been scared when I had mentioned earlier that I would send for the dogs[50]. Jezebel was not for leaving until my co-counsellor asked Tina herself to declare her destiny. Tina's declaration caused Jezebel to flee.

Another demonic spirit present in the alter ego is that of rejection, causing confusion in the person's mind to such an extent that the person can feel as though their mind will burst with pressure. Lauren Daigle sings about this in her song, "You Say"[51],

> I keep fighting voices in my mind that say I'm not enough
> Every single lie that tells me I will never measure up
> Am I more than just a song of every high and every low
> Remind me once again just who I am because I need to know
> Ooh oh
>
> *Chorus*
>
> You say I am loved when I can't feel a thing
> You say I am strong when I think I am weak
> And you say I am held when I am falling short
> And when I don't belong, oh You say I am Yours
> And I believe
> Oh, I believe
> What You say of me
> I believe
> The only thing that matters now is everything You think of me

---

50 2 Kings 9:10
51 You Say, Lauren Daigle, from album, Look Up Child 2018

In You I find my worth, in You I find my identity
Ooh oh

Chorus

Taking all I have, and now I'm laying it at Your feet
You have every failure, God, You'll have every victory
Ooh oh

Chorus

Oh, I believe
Yes, I believe
What You say of me
I believe.

Spirits of rejection compound earlier knowledge of perceived rejection, rehearsing it in the person's mind to such an extent that the person views all relationships through their lens of rejection. To them, the rejection is very real, and their accusations that others are rejecting them can cause profound hurt. This is particularly true of those who are standing with the person throughout their internal war. They must be willing to be buffeted and accused and still continue steadfastly in supporting the person.

One person reverted back to the problematic behaviour of their childhood when their alter ego surfaced. They became aware that they burst into rage when any family member or person close to them appeared to show them lack of respect but were able to control such outbursts when feeling challenged similarly by their work colleagues. It's not that they had a wrong mindset because they had their mind set on Jesus but that they had a wrong heart-set caused by an evil spirit touching their heart like lightning with a thought. It would then be expressed without warning. This is one of the ways in which the enemy contrives to bring disunity into a family, and into a church or a nation.

When anyone deceives themselves by ignoring the effects of painful events and associated emotions and thoughts, they can open the door to a spirit of deception which, in turn, makes everything seem worse. Consequently, they can lose all will to worship, to work, or even to live.

Even within an alter ego, wrong perception can arise because they want to recall only the good. One person who had been abused by her father had an alter ego who chose to remember only the good things that he had done for her. She was holding on to a part human spirit of him because she believed he was the only one who had loved her. This alter ego screamed in pain at the thought of letting him go but over time as we talked through everything, she became willing. Once God had removed this part human spirit the alter ego could readily see the full facts and was able to face them. This resolution brought that alter ego into a peace that they could never have known had the part human spirit not been removed, and it was only then that the second alter ego surfaced with the full facts and consequent rage and desire for revenge.

Consider all the above and mix in a large dose of fear and you begin to understand how enormous this battle can be for anyone with an alter ego. Only through our Father God's love and the cross of Jesus can a way be found for the person to be released from such terror and to discover what it is to live in peace and with assurance of God's faithful love. As each alter ego is healed they settle down and become loving and thoughtful, wanting to help one another.

Sometimes it is a God-inspired gift or direction that releases trauma and unknown desires. One alter ego was given a figurine of a dancer which resulted in tears flowing and a God-given picture of her as a dancer and worshipper. This led to an important healing.

Times of fun and relaxation are crucial to the overall well-being of any alter ego. One was given a blue handbag with a purse and some money. She was so excited about it that she kept bringing it out and examining it every time she surfaced for ministry so I planned when we would go shopping. Her excitement was at fever pitch and very contagious.

One day when I was out shopping, I felt strangely drawn to a particular shop. I had no idea why as I didn't want anything in it, but I wandered around trying to find out what was going on inside me. I found myself walking towards a gift section and towards some keyrings; then my attention became rivetted on a tiny lion with a full mane. I picked it up and knew somehow that I was to buy it. I learnt later that my alter ego had influenced me into buying a toy lion as a sign of the prophetic and a sign of courage. I prayed, asking Jesus to show me myself through the blood of Jesus. I saw myself letting go of a heavy backpack of "do and don't", "should and ought", "being and doing". It fell to the ground and I walked unfettered in a simple long white dress and sandals, carrying nothing. Then I heard the words, "all you need is within you". I then asked Jesus to show me the church through His blood and saw it as cleansed, joyful and in unity, walking as a bride towards Him step by step with a train which seemed to stretch for a long distance behind.

Lighter moments, even within difficult memories, often surface when most needed and are frequently prompted by Jesus. We understand so little of the spiritual world that we belong to, and so, when we learn that alter egos have been having fun together when they are below the surface, perhaps by telling a story, sharing something good, or playing a game like, I spy, we wonder at the mystery of it all.

Vital to the healing is the fact that these alter ego parts learn to live in reality and in the truth, as revealed by Jesus, and so during a time when they are fraught with pressures, unwieldy emotions, and doubts, it is helpful for them to read scripture and soak in the truths. The word of God can reach into the recesses of the heart and set any prisoner free.

One alter ego who was doing this phoned me to ask whether a particular verse was true,

> "Do not remember the sins of my youth and my rebellious ways; according to your love remember me, for you, Lord, are good." Psalm 25:7 NIV

Clearly, she was seeing hope for herself in the passage.

The Core Identity

As a consequence of the rejection and turmoil felt by an alter ego, alter egos frequently reject their identity. This is the deepest denial of all, rejecting who they really are at the core of their being, the person that God created them to be. God calls this part of a person the core identity. This process can appear similar to what happens when the inner child sets aside who they are at the core of their being in an effort to please, the part that God calls a prodigal. However, the consequences for each are different.

The act of denying our identity is rebellion against God's ordinances, even if not perceived at the time as such, and allows the enemy to take our identity captive and place a spirit of Beelzebub in its place. The person's core identity is then no longer active in their life. Beelzebub creates a new identity through speaking thoughts into the person's mind and exercising control over their actions and beliefs about themselves, generally making life miserable. The spirit assumes for itself "principal rights" over the person and dictates whatever it wants. The thoughts that come from this spirit can seem to the person at first as though they are their own, but deep within they know differently. When ministering to the alter ego of a person it is important that we be aware of the internal pressure that they have from intrusive contradictory thoughts which oppose their efforts to take every thought captive in obedience to Christ. That is not to say that they shouldn't try. Full victory will come when they choose to do so, as only then can any adverse influences from evil spirits be removed. As they learn a new way of thinking about themselves, they are released from former wrong mindsets and hearts-sets.

The effects of having a Beelzebub spirit are numerous. As mentioned already they seek to control, giving thoughts that terrify and cause confusion. These spirits attempt to indoctrinate the mind of the alter ego with lies such as "Jesus is bad", and "Lucifer gives you what you want". The alter ego may have no knowledge of Jesus, or a skewed knowledge which has been fed to them by the demonic and which completely misleads them, sometimes into being very religious.

Beelzebub spirits are heavy and dull in character and have the ability to make a person feel lethargic with a couldn't-care-less attitude. It's almost as though these spirits cut off the lifeblood and the source of joy in being alive.

Beelzebub spirits can be particularly difficult to remove, masquerading as whatever spirit they choose to be. They can be active in bringing about rejection and dissension. Their presence causes every emotion in the person to become devastatingly intense to such an extent that they can feel insane. Since Beelzebub can invite deception into the alter ego, it can magnify the intensity and pervert perception. Though primarily affecting the alter ego it affects every other part of the person. Until such time as it can be removed, some relief can be achieved for the person through binding in Jesus' name the Beelzebub spirits within each and every part of the person, and commanding them not to interfere or communicate.

One alter ego had made a covenant with a Beelzebub spirit which controlled her to such an extent that she had no will of her own. After we explained to her that God wanted her to make her own choices and reject what this spirit told her, she renounced the covenant with the spirit and chose to follow the road to truth with Jesus. However, she wanted to go to the spirit to tell it that she would not be obeying it again! We explained to her why this would be unwise as she could be taken captive again. Gradually she came into a firm knowledge of Jesus and of His desire to help her, and became confident enough in the truth to stand up against the Beelzebub spirit, resist its demands, and be delivered from it together with its influences and effects.

Another person had allowed everyone throughout life to dictate to her and "walk over her". She, also, had an alter ego who had been controlled by a spirit of Beelzebub and which had led to confusion over who God was. One day while reading a scripture with which she wasn't familiar she received revelation that she did belong to God,

> *"From birth I was cast on you; from my mother's womb you have been my God."* Psalm 22:10

This revelation dispersed the lies. Over time she came to believe that it was all right to have opinions and to choose but for a while she needed to be continually reminded and encouraged to do so.

Before a Beelzebub spirit is removed from any alter ego, the alter ego must, in Jesus' name, take back from Beelzebub any "principal rights" that this spirit has assumed for itself. In actual fact, the Beelzebub spirit never really has these since God has the principal rights to each person, but it takes advantage when a person rebels through rejecting their identity and coming into agreement with the evil spirit's influences. Once the alter ego takes back any principal rights that the evil spirit has exercised through having had control over the person, they can hand them over to God for safe keeping. It is crucial for ongoing freedom that the alter ego agree in prayer that their mind aligns with the mind of the person whose heart they belong to and that they both be aligned with the mind of Christ. This is because they remain vulnerable to suggestion from the Beelzebub spirit even after it has been evicted and is outside them.

Beelzebub spirits are pompous but become indignant if mistaken for a different spirit, so this weakness can be exploited in order to weaken them. They do not like any mention of holiness and they do not like to be made to listen to Revelation chapter 18, so reading this scripture while watching for their reactions can guide us into exactly the right time to evict them in Jesus' name.

Initially the departure of the Beelzebub spirit can leave a vacuum within the alter ego and, now that the spirit's control has gone, the alter ego can feel quite helpless and disconcerted until such time as their core identity is restored to their rightful place. In the meantime, as a form of protection for the alter ego we can pray that all Beelzebub's activities will be confounded. This is so that it cannot try to control the person from outside now that it has been evicted. Often rest and sleep help the alter ego as they are exhausted after the battle. Any confusion in their minds can now begin to be resolved and their journey into restoration continue. We are born into a world that is at war as well as possibly having a war waging within. Navigation through these stormy seas is made possible by the gentle nudging of the Holy Spirit and a knowledge of the truth in God's Word. Thanks be to God who has provided a way out through His Son.

Once the spirit of Beelzebub has left, any core identity parts can be released from their imprisonment and then may or may not appear on the surface.

They bring with them feelings of deadness, lack of purpose and hopelessness, perhaps not seeing the point in going to church if they have "anti-God" thoughts. Their thinking can be quite inflexible and include wrong perceptions and mind sets. They feel alone, rejected and not wanted because they have been isolated while in captivity. Separation from God is another factor. Only when the core identity comes to know Jesus and invite Him into their life can any isolation fade away.

One core identity part found that watching a video called, "The Miracle Maker"[52] helped her to believe. After seeing the video, she kept repeating words that she had heard in it, "Don't doubt. Believe." This helped to keep her in the truth about Jesus.

In a sense, restoration of the core identity is like being born again as the core identity leaves the dominion of darkness and comes into the light. The person has already been born again when they received Jesus, but is continuously being saved and at this point in the healing of the heart the core identity moves into the loving reality of the promise. Once a core identity returns, they need affirmation and encouragement to remain where they belong because they are used to obeying any voice and thus can easily be led back into danger. The fact that the healing of the alter egos is well under way helps, but prayer for protection can make it easier for them to stay safe.

In one person, a core identity part was very young and needed to receive teaching. She only spoke in monosyllables and had been learning colours with us. One day Jesus told her that He wanted to increase her understanding. As I waited and watched, her facial expression began to change. By the end of this session with Jesus she could add, spell, say sentences, and understand the phrase, "Are you happy?" without having to dissect it word for word. What a great teacher He is!

As part of the healing, the core identities need to be encouraged in the good things in life, as well as growing in the knowledge of what Jesus is really like and how He helps them. Above all, they need love. Taking them to places of beauty to see and enjoy the wonder of God's creation, to hear songs of worship and to experience God's goodness all contribute

---

52 *The Miracle Maker*, (animated film about the later life of Jesus), 1999, Derek Hayes and Stanislav Sokolov

to their well-being and reawaken within them the knowledge of God that they have had from creation. One core identity loved the sea and enjoyed watching ducks. One day, to her great delight, she saw a duck flying and was thrilled, but felt afraid that the good things would stop.

Core identity parts have to grow in their ability to recognise deception and self-deceptive ways. As with the alter egos, it is essential for every core identity part to pray that their mind will be one with that of Christ. As they progress, they learn what pleases God and so can bring every thought captive in obedience to Christ.

One of the consequences of spirits like Beelzebub being around until evicted is that they can affect the inner child. Don't be surprised if you are reassuring someone's inner child as well as their alter egos and core identities all at once. I was watching Frozen 2[53] recently and noted the lines, "Do the next right thing, one step at a time." What a wise instruction this is for every aspect of ministry. "Keep calm and carry on", is another useful phrase. Above all let us keep our eyes on Jesus and remain tuned in to His Spirit.

At times the pressure on all the parts, as well as on the person at the surface, can make them all long for rest and a place of peace. Sometimes one of the parts may feel miserable because of what's going on in another part or because they feel dead as a result of some spirit influencing them. They need encouragement to believe that they have a purpose and that Jesus is helping them to become free. He motivates them by telling them what specific strength they will bring to the person once intermingled. Jesus told the four alter egos in one person that their separate strengths were wisdom, courage, loyalty, and a desire to protect and care for others. This in turn heartened the person to persevere through their difficulties. In another person, one core identity was told she would bring peace while the other was affirmed in being able to see into the spiritual world. It was exciting for that person to realise that healing through integration of the parts would bring these gifts and abilities into her life in greater

---

53 Frozen 2 (2019) Disney Films

measure. It is important to nurture all parts and to encourage them to be still and rest in Jesus, abiding in Him and seeking His face.

Care has to be taken with each part in order for reconciliation of the parts and consequent blending to occur. The "dumper" (the person seeking ministry) may be afraid that hostile feelings will reappear; the alter egos may feel frightened of or feel abandoned by each other and the "dumper"; the core identities may feel isolated. There can be a whole range of issues in each that need resolution before they are intermingled. This merging is a gradual growing together, not a growing up in age followed by integration of child-parts as in fragmentation. It may feel to the person, at times, as though they are taking one step forward and two backward and, yet, this is not true. Every step takes the person forward.

At one stage we thought that the time had come for the core identity parts, who had been healed, restored and reconciled with one another, to be returned to their rightful places within the person's alter egos, and, similarly, that the alter ego parts would then gradually be assimilated into the person. It can happen this way but not always. We can never assume that we know what the next step in restoration might be, as only God knows. Life is full of surprises and nowhere more so than in the hidden mysteries of the human soul; it is therefore essential that we only minister in healing and restoration as led by God. This ministry is extremely complicated, often confusing, and we need God's wisdom to know what to do and when. This is illustrated below.

A Divided Soul appears

While focusing on healing of the heart in a specific person whom I will call Phyllis (not her real name) I was surprised, one day, while trying to comfort one of her alter egos. This alter ego was crying sorely when suddenly, a child, terrified and looking round her to get her bearings, appeared and then disappeared equally quickly. The alter ego continued releasing her anguish with agony of spirit. Eventually she became extremely tired and disappeared. That night the person hardly slept as she struggled with dreams, restlessness and pains in her stomach.

The following day this alter ego told me that the little girl who had momentarily appeared was inside her and that she herself was "sandwiched" in the middle between the person Phyllis, and this little girl. She didn't know anything about her other than that this part was angry with the adult, Phyllis.

Later, the young child appeared again, looking closely at her surroundings then at me. I could see that she was angry and, no matter what I suggested, she replied rebelliously using phrases such as, "I'm not going to do that" or "I don't like being told what to do." Because she was agitated, I tried to calm her by quietly saying, "shhh", but she thought I was ordering her to be quiet. I told her that she was safe and that no-one was coming for her but still she kept looking around in terror and began to punch her head and her body. Eventually I grasped that her head was being assaulted by a multitude of contradictory thoughts which made her feel as though it would explode. I asked God to shield her and cover her head with His helmet of protection. She cried deeply and stopped punching herself and became more peaceful. Her body then began to twitch and move because something was tormenting her within. I asked Jesus to remove whatever it was and once again she settled.

When I encouraged her to ask Jesus to help her, to my surprise she got down on the floor and prostrated herself while calling out to Him with great intensity. It was clear that something was wrong. I asked her to get up and sit beside me but she said that she had to do it this way and asked me what was going to happen to her. I suggested she ask Jesus what He would like her to do. He told her that people can sit and bow in their heart when talking to Him. She didn't understand this as she had been used to prostrating herself before satan, waiting for what he would do to her. I helped her to understand that the relationship that God wanted with her was different to that which she had known with satan. Gradually she became more relaxed and lay with her head across my knee and fell asleep.

When the alter ego returned she was very tired so we asked Jesus to take her for a rest. Phyllis came back and, later on texted me to say that she didn't have stomach pain anymore and was feeling better.

I was confused by what had happened and so turned to my only source of help, God. I reflected on what I had seen and asked God questions so that I could understand what was happening, questions like, "Where does this part belong? Who is she?" I was told that this child-part was a divided soul (chapter 1.4).

When I was with Phyllis, we asked God what had caused her to create this divided soul and why was this part only coming to light now, a long time after we thought God had finished restoring her fragmented parts. Little by little we came into understanding as God enlightened us, and as the child went through memories and released pain, hurt and terror.

This divided soul, whom we called Eve, was caused by the person fragmenting early in her life. Because of the trauma that she had been experiencing when young, she had gone into denial by rejecting the bad memories and associated emotions so that she could cope with her circumstances. This had led to her having an inner conflict between knowing the truth and denying it, and so, consequently, she fragmented as a divided soul, one part (Phyllis) continuing on in life in denial, while the other part (Eve) held the bad memories and emotions of that time. Since a divided soul child-part can be aware of what's going on in the person's life, Eve had become more and more adversely affected emotionally until she reached a stage where she intentionally collected negative emotions such as injustice, anger and hatred, and was looking towards a time when she could take revenge and make the perpetrators of her distress suffer as she had. The abuse had not only violated her soul but also her spirit at a deep level.

Not only had the abuse led to the person having a divided soul, Phyllis with Eve, but it had overloaded her heart with negative emotional upheaval which had resulted in the breaking away of part of her heart as an alter ego. Eve, with all her anger and rebellion had become buried in the alter ego. This alter ego therefore felt sandwiched between them.

As ministry continued, Eve went through memories while releasing associated emotional pain. At first, she found it difficult to receive love from Jesus because she was afraid that she would be disappointed, but gradually she relaxed and began to understand that He was different. One Sunday she agreed to attend church with me and, after a bad start in which she angrily retorted, "Get me out of here", she found the worship helpful and especially noticed a verse from the scripture reading,

"I desire mercy, not sacrifice." Matthew 12:1-4

The visiting preacher spoke on deliverance versus judgement, on mercy versus legal correctness and on not limiting what God can do by believing only within the restrictions of our humanity. He spoke of experiences that he had heard first-hand on his mission trips and, through his words of compassion, Eve came into an understanding that there were people who understood and disagreed with the kind of evil that she had encountered. It was an amazing sermon exactly at the right time for her.

Another person in whom a divided soul surfaced, while the healing of her alter ego was taking place, had been feeling angry and depressed just before this happened. We discovered that the division had been caused when she had tried to tell her mother at age nine how depressed she felt. The response had been, "You're too young to feel depressed", and so she had tried to deny the feelings. Throughout her life she had struggled against these feelings and determined not to give in to them but had never felt free from them. Interestingly this person, like the previous one mentioned, was suffering with severe stomach pain just prior to the divided soul making her appearance. I don't know whether this could be a pattern but it is cause for thought. Her healing came progressively through love and care. We melted the bindings that others had put around her will and freedom to choose, bindings that left the divided soul obligated to obey without thought for her own desires. The person who had this divided soul took responsibility for dumping on this part and gradually was restored to the freedom with which God had created her. Not long afterwards in a seminar where we were asking God to give each person revelation so as to encourage others, two people were given a picture for this person in which they saw that God had put a shield as tall as her and all around her for her protection. Not long after, this divided soul was intermingled.

Some Evidences of Deception

We always need to be on our guard against deception in its different guises. In one person a part copying a divided soul surfaced and appeared upset, maintaining that she didn't want to go through any more painful memories. Despite appearances, I felt no empathy and blamed myself for being so unfeeling towards this new arrival. I patiently explained the process towards healing and how God would take care of her but, still, I was aware that I wasn't feeling compassion or love. I just couldn't relate to her at all and was relieved when she left. The alter ego returned, feeling miserable and almost in tears. It was only as I reflected on the event that I realized that I had been coming into agreement with a demonic copy.

When I commanded it to leave in Jesus' name, the alter ego heard a mocking laugh. After seeking God, I was led to change my prayer to one asking Him to remove all demonic copies along with any spirits of deception. I heard a snarl of annoyance and the true divided soul surfaced, content and looking forward to shopping.

On a later occasion when ministering to a person who had severe rejection issues that appeared to come from an alter ego, I found myself repeating the same truths several times, and still the person would default into an entirely negative, "no-one likes me, everyone is horrible to me" default. I knew that this wasn't true but I couldn't find a way to help her to resolve her problematic thinking and was being taken on a merry-go-round. I could see how deeply the person was struggling and so I kept supporting her and ministering despite having no concrete evidence of progress. Despite asking God about what was happening it was some time before I was given insight.

Eventually, the thought, "Walter Mitty", came to mind and, when I shared this with the person, it witnessed with her and she recalled that she had lived in a fantasy world, consistently using her imagination to daydream about always being liked by everyone in the way that she believed others were. It became clear that every relationship she had fell short of her expectations.

She repented and we continued ministry. After some considerable time, I heard God tell me that she had a "self-made video." This was a new concept to me as the previous video I had experienced in ministry was a deceptive one that had been put in place by the enemy (False Video, chapter 1.5). This one was also deceptive but was a deception that the person had chosen to live in. Once we explained this to her, she repented and asked Jesus to remove it. Deep emotional pain surfaced, was released and she resumed her life of contentment.

Many divided souls are intermingled back into their host soon after they are healed. Not so with the person that I wrote about earlier who had divided souls, Phyllis and Eve. Once Eve had been released from her hurt and pain, a whole new revelation for further healing in this person surfaced,

> "He [God] reveals deep and secret things; He knows what is in the darkness, and light dwells with Him." Daniel 2:22

This is explained in the next chapter.

SECTION 3

TRAUMA HELD IN THE BODY

"For he will rescue you from every trap and protect you from deadly disease.... Do not be afraid of the terrors of the night, nor the arrow that flies in the day. Do not dread the disease that stalks in darkness, nor the disaster that strikes at midday."

Psalms 91:3, 5-6

Chapter 3:1
Releasing Trauma from the Body

*"Then they cried out to the Lord in their trouble;
he saved them out of their distresses."*
Psalms 107:13

In the last chapter I mentioned that, although the divided soul Eve had been healed, God had not intermingled her back with Phyllis as expected. Instead, we found ourselves faced with a new challenge.

We observed that at times Phyllis would lose contact with us and when we talked to her, she didn't respond. We asked God what was happening and were told, "shut down, state of altered consciousness, manifestation, something new". Once she returned to interactive awareness of her surroundings, she explained that she had been aware that we were talking to her but had been unable to respond. A memory had come to her in which she had been lying still and pretending to be asleep in the hope that no-one would come for her.

As we prayed and observed her the next time this happened, I asked her what her name was. She answered, "Me". "Me" looked like Phyllis but was afraid and somehow seemed different. We asked Jesus to take away her fear and she began to say phrases like, "It isn't fair", "No more". She was crying and sobbing deeply and saying, "I'm sorry". When we prayed for peace, Phyllis returned into full awareness once more. She remembered all that had taken place but didn't understand it.

It had become evident to us that this trauma could not be processed using any of our usual methods. Previously, we had encouraged the person in ministry to talk, draw, write, or even play with soft toys as an aid to releasing pain and restoring freedom but none of these helped the person this time. As I thought about it, I realised that these approaches were all aimed at reaching somehow into the cognitive recesses of a person's memory. If the memories couldn't be accessed cognitively, where were they? I came to the conclusion that they had become locked in her body and on asking God was told that this was so. He told us not to try and understand what had happened but to observe in what ways her body was reacting to the hidden trauma so that we could focus her on being aware of what was going on within her physically.

The next time we met with Phyllis we explained this and prayed that God would be in control of all that would take place. In Jesus' name we bound deception, delusion and illusion and rejected divination as we wanted to be sure that the enemy didn't interfere with ministry or communicate with any of us.

We asked God to bring the trauma to the surface and then took each step slowly while remaining alert to the Spirit. Phyllis began to breathe more quickly. We brought her attention to this and gently guided her towards breathing more slowly, encouraging her to take deep breaths and using the words, "breathe in.... breathe out", until her breathing settled back to normal and the effects of trauma receded. We stopped ministry and relaxed while chatting.

Tentatively, I decided to explore the topic of body trauma on the internet. I wanted to understand more about it but was aware that I must keep following the leading of the Holy Spirit while doing so. He had brought us safely through ministry thus far and He would complete the job.

On the internet there are many articles[54] that help us to understand how trauma becomes locked in the body and how it can be released. I was reassured by the fact that what I read aligned with how God had begun to guide us.

I learnt that the approach widely in use at present, called Sensorimotor Therapy, was developed by Ron Kurtz in the 1980's and was a synthesis of somatic therapy and the Hakomi method of Body-Centred Psychotherapy. Since the Hakomi method has its roots in Taoism and Buddhism, I was concerned about the wisdom of using it. However, the relational principles that proponent Pat Ogden attributes to Taoism and Buddhism are true for Christianity and not something that these other religions can claim for themselves only. The principles mentioned are, "going with the grain" (Taoism) and "gentleness, compassion and mindfulness" (Buddhism). I prayed about insights that I had gained from the articles on sensorimotor therapy and sensed that they would be helpful.

Essentially at this stage in the client's healing we were being reminded that we are spirit, soul and body and that any healing from trauma will include healing of all three. Prior to this we had been directed in how to release a person from the effects and influences of trauma in the soul and spirit, and on the emotions and heart, but now we were being faced with the need for release from trauma in the body too.

Sometimes, during times of sudden or overwhelming trauma, our cognitive processes may shut down before completing a task. From then onwards the process is waiting to be sequenced and an outcome filed away in the mind. The part of the brain where the memory had become stuck remains on the alert for anything that would indicate possible impending danger. Thus, warning signals may be repeatedly sent out to the person when perceived triggers indicate that danger is near. These triggers vary with different situations and may not appear to be connected to the trauma.

---

54   e.g., Sensorimotor Psychotherapy: A Somatic Path to Treat Trauma, Robert T Muller Ph.D., Psychology Today

As with every step forward in ministry, we asked God to be in control and that He, and only He, would be the one who brought any distress that had been locked in the body to the surface. We listened intently to the Holy Spirit and used our discernment throughout as we were aware that Phyllis was in an extremely vulnerable place. Each time we talked quietly with her encouraging her to describe what she was feeling and where she was feeling it in her body. She focussed on noticing what was happening rather than on trying to interpret it.

It seemed as though she had intense negative emotions that had been buried but which were now manifesting in her body and moving about to different parts. We encouraged her to keep tracking whatever feeling was predominant and to keep talking to us about it. At times, when she would tell us that she had a desire to push it away or take some action that she sensed would help her, we encouraged her to do this. We were aware of the strong link between fear and what she could cope with without going into panic, and so we were extremely careful to keep her safe within her window of tolerance while at the same time encouraging her to increase it in tiny steps as each negative emotion surfaced and was dispersed.

We encouraged her to follow her inclinations, releasing what she could and when she could. Sometimes she asked God to remove the troublesome emotion. When she felt that she had done enough, or when we sensed that she had, we would stop the process and relax while sharing what we had all experienced and observed. We asked Jesus to seal all healing that had taken place. Rarely did a memory come during this process.

Phyllis could recall experiencing feelings of panic throughout her childhood whenever she passed a certain place near her home but hadn't known why. Now her body was manifesting this same fear and panic and she quite naturally wanted to withdraw from experiencing it. She exercised great faith and trust in God and in us to see her through the process safely.

We observed facial expressions, body movements and what she was doing or saying, and in giving feedback helped her to gain some somatic as well as emotional control. Any statements made by us were to help her to connect with her body and not to shame or explain. Questions were aimed at helping her to stay in the process and, by not escaping into her own thoughts, remain grounded. Thus, she was helped to maintain the tracking of an emotion in her body and to regain control over it by finding her own way of dispersing it. Taking tiny steps ensured she stayed within her window of tolerance. Much of the time none of us fully understood all that was taking place at the time but discussion later helped us to understand the process. Slowly and surely, she was helped to become free and so learnt how to cope with panic in the future. The goal for each person is to replace fear and self-dependence with trust and God-dependence.

It was step by step reliance on God our Father, Jesus Christ our Saviour and Healer, and the Holy Spirit our guide that took her through the labyrinth of fear, pain and distress and out into glorious freedom.

After this experience we used this approach on several occasions to help others. Each person is unique and so their experiences and the accompanying healing processes were different. Some could remember what had caused the trauma in the first place, but hadn't been able to get free. They had come to realise that their fear and panic was often triggered when they were not expecting it and in unlikely places.

Although the insights for addressing body trauma may be used to help a person at any stage in their healing, I have chosen to put this where it belongs chronologically in our growing awareness of how we could bring freedom to the captives.

SECTION 4

TRUTH

"Train me, God, to walk straight; then I'll follow your true path. Put me together, one heart and mind; then, undivided, I'll worship in joyful fear. From the bottom of my heart, I thank you, dear Lord; I've never kept secret what you're up to. You've always been great toward me—what love! You snatched me from the brink of disaster."

Psalm 86:11 MSG

Chapter 4.1
Truth Uncovered

*"Behold, you desire truth in the innermost being,
and in the hidden part You will make me know wisdom."*
Psalms 51:6

After the release of trauma in Phyllis's body had come to an end, she and the other divided soul, Eve, were intermingled as one and named Tanya. However, this was still not the end of ministry for her.

A few days later another deeply buried, fragmented part surfaced. With hindsight we grasped that she was the last in the line of fragmented person-parts to be healed, having nowhere to dump her pain.

God ensures that His truth is preserved deep within each person, so that knowledge of Him has the potential to be restored despite the inherited consequences of sin and the traumas in life. This part held that truth along with some aspects of the true nature of horrendous abuse to which she had been subjected.

God called her, "Truth and Honesty" as she had not moved into denial but had retained the truth of who she really was. For any person who has been fragmented because of trauma there has to be a person-part that is at the end of the line with nowhere to dump any overload of pain. This part may or may not be a personal fragmentation (chapter 1.4).

Truth and Honesty had been hidden from the demonic realm so that she could only be called up by God. Once God brought her to the surface for healing the host adult, to whom she belonged, experienced a see-saw of emotions such as fear and suicidal thoughts. We talked and prayed through these as they arose.

When this child-part appeared, she was faced with the first of a number of memories of abuse, each of which caused horrific emotional upheaval. At times I was weeping and crying out to God to bring them to an end, even though I was confident that He only allowed what was necessary for her freedom and complete restoration. Since that time, I have participated in the healing of many people who have been fragmented, but it is only rarely that I have experienced signs of such extreme trauma in any one fragmented child-part. I believe that this was because she had suffered severely as a victim of continuing satanic ritual abuse. Even though most people who came to us for ministry were not faced with wickedness such as this, they did find the restoration of their final fragmentation to be difficult emotionally.

As release progressed, God replaced the name, "Truth and Honesty" with the name, "Natasha". I was thrilled by this when I discovered that one of its meanings is, "born of God". As Natasha emerged from all her horror, she radiated an inner beauty in the likeness of her Creator, and after she was intermingled with Tanya the restoration of all fragmented parts of this person was complete.

Alongside this, assimilation of her alter egos and core identities happened gradually as each forgave any "dumper", and as such "dumpers" resolved to move forward from denying their emotions to working through them with God's help.

She had become one, just as she was when God created her.

Chapter 4.2
Knowing God as the Healer of our Souls

"I pray that you may enjoy good health and that all may go well with you, even as your soul is getting along well."
3 John 1: 2 NIV

God-given emotions are Christ-centred and stable. They do not depend on people and events around us being favourable but arise from our relationship with, and knowledge of, God who is truly consistent, faithful and good towards us at all times[55]. Christ-centred emotions enable us to live consistently with a "shalom" sense of well-being, our hearts full of joy even in the difficult periods of our lives. Paul wrote that he had learned to be content in all things.[56] Lianna Klassen, in her song "Sweet Contentment",[57] uses lyrics that speak of our life journey towards this. The letter to the Hebrews exhorts us,

"Let us enter His rest." Hebrews 4:11

When we look honestly at our own heart attitudes and emotions, we may find that there are many that we want to change. We may feel anger

---

55 Jeremiah 31:3
56 Philippians 4:11
57 Love in the Ruins, Lianna Klassen, @1998, Stone Table Publishing Dawntreader Productions, Calgary, Alberta, Canada.

when thwarted, jealousy when left out, fear when confronted. Selwyn Hughes[58] writes about,

> "the importance of talking to ourselves instead of allowing ourselves to talk to us: that we must speak the truth in scripture to challenge doubts, fears, anger etc."

Martin Lloyd-Jones affirms this,

> "Have you realised that most of your unhappiness in life is due to the fact that you are listening to yourself instead of talking to yourself."[59]

Purifying our Hearts

This restoration in our journey towards ever greater freedom takes place in our souls. We can easily deceive ourselves into thinking all is well in our hearts when, in fact, we have unstable hurtful, negative attitudes and emotions buried deep within. When we realise that these have no discernible cause, and even at times don't know exactly what they are, it is time to seek God for His help. In asking God to reveal anything sinful in our hearts, He responds in love with insight, understanding and resolution.

We may be completely taken by surprise and tempted to question whether God's revelation is true but we do need to listen to the One who knows our hearts and is pinpointing something that needs to change,

> *"the heart is deceitful above all."* Jeremiah 17:9

---

58 Through the Bible in a Year, referencing Hebrews 4:12, p 1342
59 Spiritual Depression: Its Causes and Its Cure, Martin Lloyd-Jones 1965

As we release each offending emotion to Him, he exchanges it for a godly emotion, one that is stable, pure, and in line with His truth, strengthening and liberating. It is a mantle of His grace.

We can pray that the gates of our minds and hearts open wide to welcome in the King of Glory. We can ask Him to open any doors that we have closed against Him. As we invite Him in, He sweeps everywhere clean and fills our minds and hearts with His presence. As we abide in Him and in His Word, we have authority in Jesus' name over all the power of the enemy and, through knowing God, we can do great exploits.[60]

Such exchange enables us to live, no longer ruled by feelings that are the consequence of being born into a sinful world, but in the freedom that Christ has won for us at the Cross. This healing is awesome because, through it, we experience being told of many wonderful mantles that God wants to place upon us. He has so many blessings that He longs to pour out on us so that we are equipped to live in victory over the enemy, preparing the path for many to enter His Kingdom.

This transformation is accomplished through the Spirit-breathed word of God, through revelation and wisdom, and by His grace. We are encouraged to look and see, to listen and hear, to know and understand as we read, so that we can turn from our sin to Jesus and be healed. Many times in scripture, we read that those whose hearts were hardened and didn't want to turn to Jesus for healing, refused to see and hear even though they were observing and listening. The Passion Translation explains this well,

> *"I send you to this people to say to them, "You will keep learning, but not understanding. You will keep staring at truth but not perceiving it. For your hearts are hard and insensitive to me—you must be hard of hearing! For you've closed your eyes so that you won't be troubled by the truth, and you've covered your ears so that you won't have to listen*

---

[60] Daniel 11:32 KJV

and be pierced by what I say. For then you would have to respond and repent, so that I could heal your hearts." Acts 28:26-27

As we tune into the Holy Spirit, we are enabled to perceive, receive and understand so that we can be changed. Transformation of our minds and hearts is essential so that we can move in the power of God with healing and miracles. When we set our minds on the things of the Spirit and our hearts are freed from sinful attitudes, we allow greater freedom to the Spirit, allowing Him to reign in us body, soul as well as spirit. We live according to the Spirit (Romans 8: 5).

My own journey towards greater emotional wholeness was amazing in its creativity, demonstrating that God fits healing to each person in His own imaginative way. I had been struggling with feeling low in mood and completely drained of energy for some days so I asked God why this was so and was shown a picture of God pulling me up a rocky steep hill with both hands. I found the words of a question forming in my mind, "what causes me to suddenly find myself in a pit?" Immediately came the answer, "slough of despond", and with it, the recollection that this was mentioned in "Pilgrim's Progress".[61] I then had the thought, "down into hell". I prayed, asking God to release me from this pit, this "slough of despond".

A couple of days later I asked God what I had been struggling with and the words, "despair and weariness" came to mind. He told me that these emotions were like mantles resting upon me. He instructed me to "climb Jacob's ladder" and meet with Him to have these replaced by something better. I was curious as to what the reference to Jacob's ladder signified and so, to gain understanding, I read the story[62] and Jesus' reference to it[63].

---

61 Pilgrim's Progress by John Bunyan
62 Genesis 28:12 ff
63 John 1:47-50

I took up His invitation, and in the spirit climbed Jacob's ladder. There, God revealed to me that He would remove what He called, "a mantle of despair and weariness", and replace it with a "mantle of freedom" which He told me was a "mantle of the Holy Ghost". Afterwards, I felt so much better.

One night about a week after this I awoke praying but then paused in my prayer as the thought had come to me to climb Jacob's ladder. I was feeling a heavy weight on my chest and heart. Once I had quietened my soul and focussed again on God, I asked Him what was causing this heaviness. The words, "mantle of sickness and death" came to mind and, as I relinquished this, I prayed that it be replaced by a "mantle of speaking the Good News and healing the sick and setting the captives free". Once I had finished, the words "a mantle of peace and prosperity" rose up from my spirit. How encouraging!

Three days later when I was praying and worshipping with my hands raised, I had the impression that God was pulling me up closer. As I worshipped, I became aware that in Jesus I was before the throne of God and dressed in the most beautiful vibrant royal blue. I became aware that my hands felt heavy (weighty) and so I looked at them and took off my rings (physically). Then, in the spirit, I saw God put an absolutely plain ring of pure gold on my finger.

My next experience was one morning when I was feeling discouraged and God replaced this with a "mantle of hope". The following time, self-doubt was replaced by a "mantle of joy" and, in the spirit I saw a billowing cloak, gold and brightly gleaming, and had a sense of being joyful and carefree.

As I thought about the changes that were happening within me each time a mantle of ungodly emotions was replaced by a God-given mantle, I realised that not only was my soul being healed but also the distress that each negative emotion had on my spirit was removed and my sense of well-being markedly improved. It was noticeable how my love and enthusiasm for life and for the beauty of God's creation was enhanced each time God exchanged an immobilising mantle for one of His choosing. As I reflected on this in the light of different translations of 3 John 1:2, I could recognise in my own healing how interdependent my spirit, soul and body are. When our souls and spirits are "getting along well", our physical bodies have a greater possibility of "enjoying good health".

Each time that I felt despondent in the ensuing weeks I deliberately stopped what I was doing and, in the spirit, climbed Jacob's ladder and spent unhurried time seeking God for insight and release. On each occasion I simply asked God what was wrong and listened for His answer. Then I asked Him to bring the offending emotion to the surface and waited while this happened. I released it to Jesus, asking Him to remove it and give me a mantle of His choice. He would then tell me what the new mantle was.

While He was removing a "mantle of alacrity" (these words rose from my spirit) I saw myself in the spirit handing over "folded grave clothes". He then told me He was clothing me in a "mantle of zeal". This was interesting because "alacrity" means "cheerful readiness, willingness"[64] which on the surface looks positive, but I knew that this referred to the way in which I lived, jumping into action to do things for others as a consequence of learned behaviour as a child. I was doing this in my own strength and God wanted to remove that learned behaviour and replace it with His Spirit-inspired zeal.

One day I was feeling really drained while at a meeting of the Pastoral Care group. After I arrived home, I sought God for understanding and a "mantle of obstinacy" was replaced with a "mantle of long-suffering". Another day He replaced a "mantle of dread, apprehension and fear of the future" with a "mantle of faith".

---

64 thefreedictionary.com

Sometimes God gave me understanding of the exchange through words, such as "peace" replacing "striving" and at other times through pictures such as when He took away my sense of being "the fall guy" and gave me a revelation of being dressed in a multi-coloured coat like Joseph's. Another time I saw myself dressed in a gold coat and gold dust being thrown over me. Many and varied are the ways in which God meets with us with healing.

Shortly after this I was excited when, despite all my shortcomings, God invited me to ascend His holy hill,

> *"Who may ascend into the hill of the Lord? And who may stand in His holy place? He who has clean hands and a pure heart, who has not lifted up his soul to falsehood and has not sworn deceitfully."*
> Psalms 24:3-4 NASB

I then *saw* a hill which had walls offering defence at various levels on the way up. I began moving towards Jesus, wanting to bow before Him, but then became aware of a black figure beside me. When I asked about it, I was told that it was present to influence me with negative thoughts and pretexts.

After I'd asked God to remove it, I saw a very tall, shining angel, dressed in white and standing on my left where the black figure had been. He had a sword in his belt and his hand on the hilt ready to do battle. As I kept looking, I could see that I was ascending the holy hill with the angel beside me and was aware that God was using this picture to show me that there is safety and full protection for all who come to Him. I asked for impartation of the character and power of Jesus and saw a gossamer floaty mantle fall over me, a mantle of goodness and kindness. Words arose from my spirit,

> "Boldly rejoice. Take, eat (the thought came to me that God doesn't force-feed us but offers food to the hungry). The trumpet sounds. With a blast the walls will fall down. Meekness and

Majesty. Your fortifications are secure. You are ready for battle. The battle is about to begin."

Then He gave me to understand that the angel beside me was called the "Angel of the Sword" and my protection was in the "Word of Truth". God then told me that He had removed the last veil from my spiritual eyes and I would be enabled to see as He sees, the ushering in of kingdom reality through a renewed mind.

SECTION 5

LOVE

*"He is within me—I am his garden of delight.
I have him fully and now he fully has me!"*

Song of Songs 6:3 TPT

Chapter 5.1

Journey out of Fear and into Divine Love

"The one I love calls to me: Arise, my dearest.
Hurry, my darling. Come away with me!
I have come as you have asked
to draw you to my heart and lead you out.
For now is the time, my beautiful one."
Song of Songs 2:10

When I began this particular part of my own life journey, I did not know that the three days of ongoing conversation with God would prepare me to receive a physical healing that I had been asking for over many years. In sharing the incredible lengths to which God went to, demonstrating His mercy and grace, I hope that you will be encouraged to seek dialogue with Him too.

I had been asking God for many months for a baptism of fire and was on this occasion spending time quietly with Him when these thoughts arose from my spirit,

> "A power house. Return to Me. Open the door for My mercy. Make Me a channel of your peace. Watch and wait. Take My words forth to the nations. Humble yourself before Me and I will exalt you. Be faithful in prayer, lacking nothing. Hold yourself

ready for what I am about to do. Take the sword of the Spirit which is the Word of God and go boldly where I proclaim. Take My Word to the nations and do not be fearful. I have equipped you and mentored you. You are ready. Moved with compassion."

Much of this seemed outside my world of possibility as I was perpetually plagued by fearfulness and preferred to be in the background. I pondered whether taking His word to the nations could be referring to the fact that He had asked me to write a book about the ministry of His Father heart. He responded to my thoughts,

"Take My Word wherever you go and don't hesitate. I am with you always and where My Word goes it never fails."

"Lord," I responded, "I need you to verify this". As I continued pondering these things, I sensed what seemed like an unmistakable request from God,

"Fast for three days."

Surprised, I listened further. Then came the words,

"A spiritual fast, only My Word."

I knew He was referring to the scriptures but didn't know where to start.

"Where?" I asked.

"Song of Songs" was the response.

Inwardly I had a sinking feeling because this was a book that I found difficult to understand and it was certainly not my favourite. I set aside three consecutive days in which I could devote myself to this.

The night before I was to begin, I awoke with a deep sense of apprehension. There had been a tightness in my chest for nearly three weeks and it had been increasing. It had intensified one night when I was walking my dog past a certain house and a woman had yelled at me for no obvious reason. This was repeated on my return journey home and so I had gone to her door to find out what was wrong but she didn't answer. The next time that I was out walking, I was too frightened to pass her house and so I took a different route. Now I asked myself whether this pain in my chest was arising out of fear of confrontation. I was well aware that fear of man had plagued me in so many ways throughout my life, and although greatly lessened, it was still present to some extent. I prayed that God would remove everything from my life that was shakeable, and the words, "apostle Paul" came to mind. I reflected on his being struck with blindness thus demonstrating his true spiritual state, and wondered whether these difficulties in my life revealed some sort of blockage within that was holding me back from yielding myself more fully to God, a hindrance that only God could bring into the light and remove. I have noticed many times in ministry to others that, when God is about to heal a person, the difficulties which they struggle with may intensify. Maybe God intended to use these three days to cleanse me from fear? Recently in a television broadcast I had heard Roberts Liardon[65] say,

> "We must continue in Christian bravery to confront the evils of our time and keep advancing the Christian borders with no shame, no embarrassment. Come out of your fear. Come out of your prisons. And this time preach like a man on fire, a woman on fire and don't apologise for who or what you are. God called you. He will defend you, back you up. You need not be compromised. But, above all things, let the Spirit of God infuse your spirit that you become a mighty man of God, a mighty woman of God. God will use you if you'll be available and not be afraid."

---

65 Roberts Liardon is a Christian speaker and author of many books including Run to the Battle, 1989

It seemed to me that his words were spoken directly to me. As I prayed about the severe pain in my chest, the words, "enshrine" and, "Bel stoops down" came to mind. One of the definitions of "enshrined" is,

> "preserve [preservation of] a right, tradition or idea in a form that ensures it will be protected and respected e.g., in a treaty, construction; mindset of loyalty, fear inspired, subservience; immortalise." [66]

I wondered whether I had a belief system that was "enshrined" within me and had arisen out of fear. Faced with the thought that I was letting fear rule in my life, I asked, "Is this idolatry?" and from deep within my spirit came the words,

> *"casting down every imagination and false pretension that raises itself against God."* 2 Corinthians 10:5

I asked the Holy Spirit to help me to change my thinking and develop a mindset in line with that of Jesus.

I then reflected on the words,

> *"Bel stoops down."*

GOD'S WORD® translates this verse,

> *"The god Bel bows down; the god Nebo stoops low. Their statues are seated on animals and cattle. The gods that you carry are burdens, a load for weary people."* Isaiah 46:1

Certainly, my fear was a burden to me and this seemed to be pointing once more to the fact that I bowed to fear. It was like an idol in my life.

---

66 Oxford English Dictionary

In order to try and cope I had developed a false identity. Colossians 3:10 (NASB) came to mind,

> ".......and have put on the new self who is being renewed to a true knowledge according to the image of the One who created him...."

This confirmed my thoughts. I needed renewing in my soul to become more like Jesus.

A question came to mind, "Lord", I asked, "are there gaps in my faith?"

The answer came, "Intellectualism, dogma, unbelief".

Slowly I pondered each word. "Dogma" is defined as,

> "a principle or set of principles laid down by an authority as incontrovertibly true. It serves as the primary base for a belief system and it cannot be changed or discarded without affecting the very system's paradigm." [67]

If I had a belief system that was based on ungodly dogma then I wanted to know. I asked, "Is there any dogma that I have 'bought into' that isn't Yours? Lord, show me where my thinking is aberrant, please." I returned to Colossians 3 and verses 1-3 (NASB),

> "Therefore, if you've been raised up with Christ, keep seeking the things above, where Christ is, seated at the right hand of God. Set your mind on things above, not on things that are on earth. For you have died and your life is hidden in Christ."

It wasn't until healing of my heart had taken place over the following three days of the spiritual fast that God returned to these insights to address them specifically. At this stage He was showing me His goal - that I serve God and not fear, that I be free from fear of man.

---

67 Oxford English Dictionary

Healing 1

The first stage of stepping out of my imprisonment to fear was to reject the false self that I had created because of fear. I wanted God to restore my true core identity to her rightful place.

I opened my Bible at Song of Songs 1:1,

> *"May he kiss me with the kisses of his mouth."*

If I was supposed to see this as God with me, I just could not get it. I didn't even like it as I had no spiritual understanding at that time about what it truly meant. I continued reading and, as I read the request,

> *"Take me with you, let's run"*

I knew that resistance was rising up within. In my head I wanted to identify with this but deep within me I did not. Why was this? In searching for an answer, I found myself writing down some of my characteristics and as I did so I began to realise that they belonged to a "me" that had been manufactured in order to please others. Already God was pointing to issues that He intended helping me to be free from. I found it easy to give others time but not to receive it from others. I found it easy to love others and have compassion on them but difficult to receive it for myself. Internally I had a battle between perceived respectability and abandonment to love. I knew this was a generational issue. The words,

> *"They made me a caretaker of the vineyards, But I have not taken care of my own vineyard."* Song of Songs 1:6

resonated with truth for me personally and set me thinking again. I had never felt special to people and thought I was only liked in as much as I was useful and devoted my life to helping them. Reading on, I paused at these words which rang true for me,

> *"Why should I wander like a non-entity? Why should I stay in the shadows?"* Song of Songs 1:7

My own rejection of my true self meant that I had buried the "me" that I was created to be and was using a false identity based on what I perceived others expected. I was wandering like a non-entity.

Then a question formed in my mind, "What is pure love?" I thought about our Heavenly Father who loves us because He is love, not because of any need that He has. I thought about how Jesus provides for my need out of His love for me, not because of what I can do for Him.

So many of us are full of fear and afraid of rejection. God tells us that perfect love casts out fear[68] but how do we receive the perfect love our Father God offers when we reject it because we fear rejection? I didn't know the answer but I did what I knew I had to do. I repented, rejecting my faulty thinking and behaviour, and asked God to show me the true me that is made in His image, my true core identity, so that I could walk in freedom with Him.

Rising from my spirit came the words,

> "Rise up, O men of God!"
> "Rise up O, men of God!
> Have done with lesser things.
> Give heart and soul and mind and strength
>
> To serve the King of Kings."[69]

I continued reading,

---

68   1 John 4:18
69   Excerpt from Hymn by William Pierson Merrill, 1911

> "He has brought me to His banqueting hall and his banner over me is love" …. "Do not awaken love until the time is right." Song of Songs 2:4,7 TLB

I wondered when the time would be right and *decided to read this verse in the NIV,*

> "Do not arouse or awaken love until it so desires."

This translation helped me to understand that the time had to do with God's timing but also with my willingness. I sensed that I had buried my ability to receive love because of fear of rejection; so I asked God to awaken love within me for me, my true self, my core identity. A child expects and believes they are totally loved unless something happens to destroy this.

The words, "jettison the false self" came to me. This I chose to do. I then recalled the words, "moved by compassion" which had come to me two days previously. I knew that this compassion was an attribute of God (Spirit Love, Unveiling our True Identity in Christ, chapter 1.2), an aspect of His pure love, and that it is different from responses initiated for the wrong reason whether out of pity, compulsion, manipulation, guilt, or self-fulfilment. I had never considered that the love that I demonstrated to others was anything other than an expression of genuine love. Now, here, I was being faced with my vulnerability and sinfulness.

I continued praying, "Lord, please show me the 'me' created in Your own image. Give me revelation of who I really am." I then turned to the same Scripture again and read the words, this time in the NASB translation,

> "Do not arouse or awaken my love until she pleases."

I thought about how it might apply to me. Since I was the one who had adapted my life to what I thought would give me acceptance, I was the one who had rejected my own core identity. I needed to prepare myself to welcome this part of me back. Only God could transform me so that this part of me was free to return to her rightful place, her "place in this world". He began to reveal to me how much He loves me, through many scriptures that came to mind. Little by little He was helping me to move away from my self-effacing thinking and into truth. I read on,

> *"Arise, my darling, my beautiful one and come along. For behold, the winter is past, the rain is over and gone. The flowers have already appeared in the land; the time has arrived for pruning the vines, and the voice of the turtle dove has been heard in our land. The fig tree has ripened its figs, and the vines in blossom have given forth their fragrance, Arise, my beautiful one, and come along! O my dove, in the clefts of the rock, in the secret place of the steep pathway."* Song of Songs 2:10-14

I pondered the word "dove". It is a symbol of purity and was a sign of the Holy Spirit coming down upon Jesus at His baptism. God calls us to fly to Him, into a secret and quiet place of safety. So often we look for Him through attending conferences and reading books rather than simply seeking Him in quietness. I began to reflect on what Jesus is like and how much I wanted to fellowship with Him.

I was about to pray about the false self (forgetting that I already had) and, as I closed my eyes, I saw an enormous white dog with a black collar sitting on its haunches. I immediately thought, "black dog, white dog" and sensed that the black dog (my false self) had gone. The white dog was my core identity - my true self - but what did the black collar mean? It was only later that I was given understanding.

God was calling me to a new level of obedience, calling me to put Him first and not be distracted. A fierce determination is needed to lay hold of the Kingdom of God. The thought came,

"Don't let anything disturb the season in which you are seeking Me to a new level. Seize My word and don't let anything else in."

I sensed a need to read about Saul's conversion in Acts 9. As a light shone around him, he was rebuked by Jesus and struck with blindness. He was then instructed to wait. During this time, he was given a vision of Ananias and told what would happen. Just as he had been shown, Ananias arrived where Paul was staying and prayed for him to receive the Holy Spirit whereupon Paul received his sight back.

As I thought about Paul's three days of blindness, I was reminded of Jonah, who spent three days in the belly of a fish because he had not wanted to follow God's instruction to go and preach repentance to the people of Nineveh who were in spiritual darkness[70]. At the end of the three days Jonah was expelled out of the darkness of the fish and did as he had been commanded. Only then did Nineveh repent and come out of her spiritual darkness. I then recalled that Jesus had been subjected to spiritual darkness for our sakes, and was then resurrected. Now, here I was fasting on scripture for three days, three days when the dark places in my life were being exposed and removed so that light could enter. I was amazed.

A passage from Isaiah 51 came to mind, one that had held significance for me some years earlier; so I decided to read through the chapter. Two verses resonated with me,

> "Soon, all you captives will be released." Isaiah 51:14

and

> "I have put my words in your mouth
> and hidden you safely in My hand." Isaiah 51:16

I asked, "Lord, am I out of the prison of fear?" and had the thought, "an escapee".

I then began to ask lots of questions. It wouldn't be like me not to!

---

[70] Jonah 1:17

"Lord, please give me a revelation of how You see me, a revelation of the attributes of my core identity."

Some attributes of a person may be buried within a person-part and I wanted to know what changes I could expect once my true identity was restored! I asked, "What are You leading me into? What is the confirmation of the prophecy?"

Although I didn't think of it at the time, removal of fear was paving the way for fulfilment of the prophecy. These words came to me,

"Rest assured. All will be revealed. It's a matter of time. Three days and He rose again."

God was assuring me that the revelation would come with my life being resurrected in some way at the end of the three days.

Suddenly, I had a picture of a baby's head emerging from the womb. I felt shock. What did it mean? The word, "re-birth" seemed associated with the picture. Had part of me been imprisoned by my fear of man and was now being re-birthed? At the revelation of the baby being birthed, I sensed the words,

"Not by might, nor by power but by My spirit." Zechariah 4:6

and that I was witnessing a re-birth, a spiritual birthing of some part of me. I asked, "Is this the re-birth of my core identity, my real self?" and had the thought, "mineshaft" (a vertical or horizontal shaft to remove something). It was the next day before I had confirmation as to what this meant. This re-birth or being born into life was certainly my core identity being restored to her rightful place in my life. I chose to welcome her back into full participation in my life and asked God to mingle us together so that we might never separate again.

I repeated my previous question in different format. Sometimes doing this opens the door to an answer,

> *"Lord, what qualities am I receiving through her presence?"*
>
> *"Faithfulness, loyalty, integrity…*
>
> *joy-filled, abandonment, gregarious, zealous, free, courageous, whole-hearted, true.*
>
> *She will break down barriers, open the way. Her words will be few and concise but will be spoken with power. She can go with the flow but if things get extreme, she can deal with it."*

I was amazed and excited. There were qualities there that certainly hadn't been aspects of my character up until then. As I write I marvel at what God told me then. I have indeed changed from being a very quiet person to being quite gregarious, to the point that I sometimes think I need to be quieter. I am free from the need to be a people-pleaser. God is amazing.

I then began to read Nehemiah and was struck by the fact that he prayed, asking God that the king would give him favour "today". He must have continued praying because it was five months before the king queried his sad countenance and, having ascertained the reason, gave him permission to see to the issue concerning him: the rebuilding of the walls of Jerusalem. I noticed, too, that when the king did remark on his sadness and asked what was wrong, Nehemiah was terrified!

Healing 2

In this part of my healing, I was released from some of the effects on my life of having been controlled and full of fear. I was given revelation that a further measure of faith had been released within me. I was released from anger and the influence of antichrist spirits which had been at the root of my fear of authority.

I was excited to find out what the new day would unfold. My chest still felt pressure and when I was told of someone who was in hospital, panic and fear rose up and the pressure on my chest got worse. This confirmed that the chest problem had been associated with fear and apprehension, and that God had been surfacing it for some days now. Maybe today it would finally go. Words rose up from my spirit,

> *"God is my refuge and strength so I will not fear."* Psalm 46:1

The thoughts continued to flow,

> *"His Spirit brings me joy. The joy of the Lord is my strength. God lives in me and is my Protector. I cannot be destroyed. Be still and know God. He is my fortress."*

Gradually the fear lessened. Isaiah chapter 51 came to mind and I read the opening words,

> *"Listen to Me all who hope for deliverance - all who seek the Lord! Consider the rock from which you were cut, the quarry from which you were mined. Yes, think about Abraham, your ancestor, and Sarah, who gave birth to your nation. Abraham was only one man when I called him. But when I blessed him, he became a great nation."* Isaiah 51:1, 2 (NLT)

I stopped in my tracks because I had been reminded of the word, "mineshaft", from the previous day. I sensed joy in my spirit at confirmation that the re-birth of the previous day had indeed been of my true self, a child of Abraham, man of faith. I asked the question, "Is my true identity, that has been brought up the "mineshaft", like Abraham and full of faith?" Abraham is the spiritual father of those who have faith (Romans 4:11). Even when there was no physical reason for hope, Abraham kept on hoping, believing that he would become the father of many nations[71]. Abraham's faith did not weaken even though at a hundred years of age, he reckoned his body was as good as dead, as was Sarah's womb. The words of Disney's song "Let it go"[72] came to mind. I looked up the lyrics and honed in on two lines which seemed to describe how I had lived,

> "Don't let them in, don't let them see,
> Be the good girl you always have to be
> Conceal, don't feel, don't let them know
> Well, now they know
> Let it go, let it go
> Can't hold it back anymore."

Suddenly someone came to mind and the tightness and pain in my chest increased. I started to rebuke fear, panic, anxiety, procrastination, bitterness - the words just flowed from me without my thinking about them. I wondered whether the fear I had experienced all my life had anything to do with the apprehension that I had felt whenever I was near this person of authority. The word, "forklift'" had come to mind and I recalled feeling, throughout my life, that it was as if I had been lifted up and put down wherever it suited others. I could understand why this word described how I had felt as a child. The words of the song continue,

> "Let it go, let it go
> Can't hold it back anymore
> Let it go, let it go."

The pain of sadness and sorrow over how it had been, came over me. Waves of sobbing and the pain of heartache rose up within me and were released as I "let it go".

---

71 Romans 4:18
72 From the film, "Frozen", Walt Disney's Pictures, 2013

As I reflected on what had happened, I understood how this fear of authority had imprisoned me in so many ways; in relationships, and while speaking or teaching in front of people. It had been crippling. All through my life I had fought internally to overcome it but had never managed to get free. Gradually through years of healing in my emotions it had lessened but the root had still been there. I hoped that this would be the end of it.

I began to declare my freedom. "I am free to choose! My choices are my choices and are right for me, even if others don't agree! I can live! I can be me! I believe that I can succeed! My thoughts, beliefs and capabilities are not second rate nor to be walked over! I rise up in the Name of Jesus!"

Suddenly, I heard the words, "Step out of the crate!" I thought about whether that described how I had felt as I was growing up: being lifted and laid wherever it suited those who had influence over me. I was reminded of the word, "forklift". In response, I prayed for the freedom to be who I am without fear while, in my mind, stepping out of the crate. I declared, "I walk free". I then asked God to help me to live in freedom and to embrace His glorious love. All His healing is grace, grace, grace. I am so profoundly thankful to My Father of grace. I relaxed into worship.

After a while I asked the part of me that is my core identity to show me what she knew about My Heavenly Father. Although she had been denied freedom to experience this life, she had never been separated from Him by life's ongoing difficulties. From my spirit rose the words,

"There is no shadow of turning with Him." James 1: 17

I then sensed God was speaking these thoughts,

"I am the Good Shepherd who tends His sheep and My sheep hear My voice and obey it. Walk tall, My child. Be proud of your inheritance. You are in the hands of Almighty God before whom there is no

shadow of turning. All His good gifts are yours - restoration, healing, salvation, mighty works. You are the clay. I am the potter. I have prepared you for this day. You will succeed in My calling to you and bring My light to the nations. You are My mouthpiece for good. Your words will transform the hearts of many. Enjoy Me and be free to enjoy the life I've given you - gay abandon, joy everlasting, love in abundance, hope overflowing, faith in Me. Walk steady and do not fear, only trust. My light will rise over you with healing in its wings. Do not be faint-hearted but rejoice. Your salvation is unfolding. A new day is dawning. A day of hope (I saw brightness at this point). Be courageous, My little one. You are in the shadow of the Almighty from whom comes your aid."

I handed over the self-limiting that had arisen from thinking of myself as, "second best", and declared I would move without limit in whatever God wanted. I asked, "Lord, what are You preparing me for?"

"Before councils."

was the response. I was reminded of the words,

"I will give you the right words and such wisdom that none of your opponents will be able to reply or refute you." Luke 21: 15 (NLT)

The passage continues,

"For even those closest to you will betray you. They will even kill some of you. And everyone will hate you because you are My followers. But not a hair of your head will perish!

By standing firm you will win your souls."

I thought about the followers of Jesus and how they were persecuted and killed. Sometimes it is difficult to understand exactly what Jesus is saying but the bottom line is that He calls us to trust Him no matter what. As I waited, I heard the words,

"You will stand."

and recalled that someone had declared this over me about twenty years previously. The words continued,

"Take meat for today, and tomorrow you stand. Accept the bread of heaven meekly. Devour My Word for from it flow the wellsprings of life. You are My beloved and you reign and rule with Me. Take the cudgel. You will wield it with My words of wisdom and might. I am sure-footed, and I will teach you what you must say."

I asked, "Lord, is it time to write the book?" The reply came,

> "In writing it you will form your thoughts and hear My Word and be prepared. It is for you a source of Me, My wisdom over the years. It is water to the thirsty and bread to the weary. You are on the threshold."

I realised that God was telling me that writing about my journey with Him was for my sake, and to prepare me for the road ahead, as well as to encourage others. I had been given a gift of a devotional book at Christmas and, now, felt an urgency to read the meditation for that day,

"I am able to do beyond all you ask or imagine. Come to Me with positive expectations knowing that there is no limit to what I can accomplish. Ask My Spirit to control your mind so you can think great thoughts of Me. Do not be discouraged by the fact that many of your prayers are yet unanswered. Time is a trainer, leading you to wait upon Me and teaching you to trust Me in the dark. The more extreme your circumstances, the more likely you are to see My power and glory at work. Instead of letting difficulties draw you into worrying, try to view them as setting the scene for My glorious intervention. Keep your eyes and your mind open to all that I am doing in your life." (Ephesians 3:20,21; Romans 8:6; Isaiah 40:31; Revelation 5:13)[73]

---

[73] Sarah Young, "Jesus Calling" (2011), January 6th

The thought came, "ask Me how I see the world". Then these words flowed,

"Dog eat dog (defined as destructive, ruthless competition without self-restraint). This is what is happening in this world. Not so in My Kingdom. Light versus darkness. Shine like lights in this dark world. Radiate hope. All creation's straining to see the sons of God come into their own. Mark My words, 'Less is more' in this busy world. Be still and know that I am God - God of the universe which I created by My hand and the Word of My mouth. Kingdoms come, and kingdoms go but My Word lasts forever. Humble yourselves under the mighty hand of God and I will bring you peace."

A thought came to me, "Lord," I asked, "Have I been subjected to anger?"

Back came the answer,

"Multiple fractures."

In the spirit I saw a surface with multiple cracks radiating from a hub where a fist had landed in anger. "How is this healed?" I asked.

"Through My love. Believe and receive My love."

"Will You give me a scripture, please, that shows Your love heals a fractured heart?" The response came,

"You will leap like a deer."

I thought of the words,

> *"The sovereign Lord is my strength. He makes me as sure-footed as a deer, able to tread upon the heights."* Habakkuk 3:19

then I was reminded of the leaping of calves mentioned in Malachi,

> *"But for you who fear My Name, the Sun of righteousness will rise with healing in his wings. And you will go free, leaping with joy like calves let out to pasture. On the day when you act, I will tread upon the wicked as if they were dust under your feet, says the Lord of Heaven's armies."* Malachi 4: 2,3

The response continued,

> "Surround yourself with beauty, peace in My presence. Take time to be restored in My grace. Enjoy space. Listen to the birds, My creation. Take My yoke. Come unto Me all you who are weary and carry heavy burdens and I will give you rest. Take My yoke upon you. Let Me teach you because I am humble and gentle at heart and you will find rest for your souls. For My yoke is easy to bear, and the burden I give you is light."

As I reflected on this conversation, I was reminded that during that time, whenever I thought about doing ministry my chest would tighten. I was still anxious at heart but why? Martha and Mary came to mind; Martha who was anxious about "many things" and Mary who chose "the better way". Perhaps, I was under pressure from doing too much. "Lord," I asked, "Am I to take a break from ministry?" The reply came,

> "Take a rest."

"Lord, can we finish each ministry first and then I will not take on any more at present?" He responded,

> "My will."

The conversation continued, back and forth, "What's Your will?"

> "Rest. Be content. Stop striving."

"Lord, will You give me insight for each person in ministry please? Can I continue periodically with (various names followed relating to the ministries I was presently engaged in)?"

> "Wind them up. Have them seek My face. There's turmoil inside you. Be still until it settles. It is My will that you should rest. I love you as much as the others. I am Saviour. I am Healer. They can look to Me. Gross misconduct."

Shocked, I said, "What? What are You referring to?"

> "Dependency. Some want to be pointed in the right direction. Some want to be carried. Some want to carry. Your purpose is to point the way, both in Me and to Me. You point them to Me to seek Me and point them in the right direction through knowledge and wisdom. You can teach them but don't carry them."

I was reminded of a scripture from Isaiah 30:20,

> *"Though the Lord gave you adversity for food and suffering for drink, he will still be with you to teach you. You will see your teacher with your own eyes."*

The inner voice continued,

> "Prepare your notes. Write your book. That will suffice. That will serve to point the way. Write it like a diary, demonstrating how to follow the Shepherd's voice as He reveals His Father's heart: demonstrating how to talk to, listen to and walk with Father God; how to follow My path to recovery and freedom. My sheep need to hear My voice."

I responded, "Lord, I need further help please. It feels like a daunting task to write in a way that is not just a set of guidelines and instructions but gives glory to You." As I listened quietly, these words came to me,

"It will be My love letter to the hurting, showing them how they can walk away from pain and walk into My arms. Truly, Beloved, how can it be any other way? Not by might, nor by power but by My Spirit. Remember the baby who was birthed yesterday?"

Later, when I was reading this over again, I saw myself leaping on the hills following the Shepherd. Truly all that I was reading in Song of Songs was coming to pass for me. Over time, I began to grasp that I would write the book like a diary in the sense of writing it as a personal reflection which would be chronological in nature, each chapter describing a process in ministry and positioned relative to the others according to the order in which I was taught by the Holy Spirit. Insights would be illustrated by examples which had been gathered together from various times over the period.

To-day, as I was reading in John's Gospel,

> *"Then Jesus said to those Jews who believed Him, 'If you abide in My word, you are My disciples indeed. And you shall know the truth, and the truth shall make you free.'"* John 8:31-32 NKJV

the thought came to me that this verse was taking place in my life. As I was spending time with God and in His Word, I was being set free. Jesus truly is,

> *"the Bread of Life."* John 6:35

It was now evening and I asked, "Lord, is there anything You want me to think about now?" From my spirit came the words, "Robbing Peter to pay Paul" and so I asked the question, "Is this in me?" to which I got the reply, "A franchise."

"A franchise is an authority that is given by an organization to someone, allowing them to sell its goods or services or to take part in an activity which the organization controls."[74]

It seemed to me that God was pointing to something outside me that had some authority over my life, perhaps demonic in nature. I asked God, "Does Paul ("Robbing Peter to pay Paul") represent a demonic spirit?" He replied, "The perceived supplier". I asked, "Is there some entity demanding reward for 'help' given?" He replied, "Holding to ransom".

I find that when I'm trying to understand what God is revealing to me that I ask lots of questions until I fully grasp what God is conveying to me and understand what is being healed or restored and how it will take place. Sometimes God's responses are not direct answers but, even then they are His way of keeping me on His track. Although I was pondering and asking God questions as I read slowly through Song of Songs, I was also being directed to or reminded of other scriptures which I would then read in a similar way. Later when this period of "fasting for three days" was complete, I used the back of a roll of wallpaper to write out what had taken place during the time. I had a column with the scripture references and a column with insights and prayers. What really thrilled me was to discover how closely God had used the scriptures to initiate a conversation which led to a specific healing, and how often those scriptures matched the process.

At this stage in my most recent conversation with God, I was struggling to understand exactly what He wanted to reveal to me. I was thinking that Peter referred to my real self and Paul referred to a demonic spirit who was the "perceived supplier". This demonic spirit, or entity, was holding someone to ransom. The picture of the white dog with the black collar came back into my mind. I knew that the white dog was my true identity but still didn't know what the black collar was. Perhaps the black collar represented some control that was being exerted over my core identity? Perhaps it represented control being exerted by some

---

74 Collins Dictionary

demonic spirit which was holding my core identity to ransom? The thought came to mind, "Is there an antichrist spirit pulling the strings?" to which I sensed the response, "He is in the background orchestrating through people. He has the 'franchise'." I asked, "What made my true identity hide away?" "Terror", came the reply.

As I continued praying, I recalled that God had shown me several years previously that, as a baby in the pram, I had sensed something that had scared me. He had told me that what I had sensed was an antichrist spirit and that this had invoked terror within me. At the same time my dad had been angry because I was crying. Now, I could understand why I had a learned response of terror when faced with any opposition or anger towards me. The fact that the terror had been buried within my identity part meant that it remained buried until that part was surfaced and only then could the terror be released. This would perhaps explain why I never could get completely rid of the fear that plagued me over the years. My thinking now was that "Peter" definitely referred to my true core identity and "Paul" to antichrist spirits outside me.

Because I had become so frightened of authority figures in my life, I had learnt ways in which to lessen confrontation like people-pleasing and never standing up for myself. Thus, I had denied who I really was, the person that God had created me to be, and so had manufactured a false identity. Now, although my false identity had been removed, my true identity could still be controlled by any antichrist spirit that was near me. In this way antichrist spirits continued to "hold the strings", controlling my true identity through fear. This had been symbolized by the black collar round the neck of the white dog.

In Jesus' Name, I chose to be free and asked God to take the collar off my core identity so that she could walk free, no longer influenced adversely by any antichrist spirit. In the spirit I could sense her clapping and jumping. I then asked, "Lord, would you remove any emotion of fear, apprehension, or panic and replace it with Your peace, please?" I sensed an explanation through the words,

> "Ravaged over time, savaged, a non-entity."

and knew that this was how I had thought of myself and why I had behaved as I did. Then I heard the words,

> "Her Name is Sarah - mother of many."

At this I felt such peace and reassurance because God had called me by this name many years previously, as I was ministering to the many child-parts of several people who were fragmented. These child-parts had looked on me as their "mother". Then I heard the instructions,

> "Roll the stone away. Take off the grave clothes. Step out into the light. You are free."

As I shut my eyes and thanked God, I saw the upper part of a snake with its head towards me but the head was hanging down. Its head was flat and its tongue kept darting in and out of its mouth and the thought came to me, "It can't touch me. Its tongue is darting in and out but it can't touch me. Nothing shall harm me. God is my witness". Then I heard the words,

> "Here ends the first lesson."

I asked, "What is the first lesson?" The response was,

> "Snakes cannot harm you."

I recalled the passage where Jesus says,

> *"Behold, I give you the authority to trample on serpents and scorpions, and over all the power of the enemy, and nothing shall by any means hurt you."* Luke 10:19

and realised that this would include any antichrist spirits that had been affecting me. They couldn't harm me, and I had authority over them in the Name of Jesus. God was affirming me as a weapon in His hands to remove these spirits when He asked.

In summary, at this stage my false identity had left and my true identity been restored and set free, and I had been given understanding about where my battle with fear really lay, together with the way in which to deal with it. I had also been receiving the love of my Father deeper and deeper into my heart. His love was truly removing the fear.

Healing 3

Further healing in my heart. Release from a familiar spirit and from the word, "catastrophic" written over my life, from bitterness, resentment and fear (yet again!). The garden in my heart.

To-day, God directed my attention to what we know as a familiar spirit. This is an evil spirit which is passed down a generational line and is so familiar to members of the family that it often goes unnoticed. It can influence thought processes and attitudes. When I asked how this was affecting me, I heard, "fear and trembling, catastrophic, Lucifer, madman". Then a verse came to mind,

> *"With joy you shall draw water from the wells of salvation."* Isaiah 12:3

God always encourages us when we are in the middle of anything negative. He was showing me that as I drank from the wells of salvation, I would experience joy in the working out of my salvation,

> *"My beloved ones, just like you've always listened to everything I've taught you in the past, I'm asking you now to keep following my instructions as though I were right there with you. Now you must continue to make this new life fully manifested as you live in the holy*

awe of God—which brings you trembling into his presence. God will continually revitalize you, implanting within you the passion to do what pleases him." Philippians 2:12-13 TPT

Sometimes we do not understand specifically what is meant by a revelation, but if we remain close to the actual wording at such times, we can be confident that God will use our trust in Him to accomplish His purpose. I didn't have difficulty in understanding why the phrase, "fear and trembling" could be a family trait. I knew it had been within me and I could recall occasions when I had witnessed it operating in other members of the family. I also could understand the presence of a Lucifer spirit influencing my family line because of religiosity (Unveiling our True Identity in Christ, see section 2, chapter 2.7) in previous generations. I hadn't been aware that the word, "catastrophic" was outworking in the family but I was prepared to sever myself from it and its influences and effects. The word, "madman" didn't seem relevant but I wasn't going to ignore it! I readily renounced and rejected all of these from my life in the Name of Jesus. Having done that, I got the impression that my heart was locked with bitterness, resentment and fear inside, and so, in the spirit, I gave the key to Jesus to open the door, go in and cut down the thorns and briers, and burn them (these words were flowing from the Holy Spirit through my spirit as I prayed). I asked again for a baptism of fire. In the spirit I could see Him enter and destroy the thorns and briers, and then He planted a garden. I was fascinated. It was a garden in which He would walk with me and it had a garden seat for two where we could sit and talk. "My garden of love", He said.

I recalled that about thirty years previously God had given me an impression of a garden while inviting me with the words, "Come into the garden with Me". In this picture I could see through a wrought iron gate that the garden was full of tall, bright colourful flowers such as delphiniums and foxgloves and that there was a path winding its way through them. This picture had come to mind several times over the years and I had even hunted for something similar on the internet but had never found an exact representation. Now here I was again, looking at the garden and God revealing that it was the garden in my heart. I asked Him what He was planting and these came to mind, "pomegranates, lilies, sunflowers, thistles" (*this last one seemed odd but I could sense His humour as He honoured my Scottish heritage*), "forget-me-nots, tulips, sage, heathers, grasses, marigolds, pansies, daffodils, candytuft, roses…" As I watched, He created paths to walk on and places to sit. The words continued, "a bower; the secret place of the Most High". Words from a familiar song arose in my spirit,[75]

> I hear You're in the business of healing hearts
> That's why I've come though
> I don't even know where I should start
> I've tried a thousand places, cried a million tears
> But nothing ever met my need and no-one ever calmed my fears
> Only you can reach me there
> Only you can heal, and my prayer,
> Is that by Your Spirit You might reveal
> The part of my heart that You need to heal.
> Well, the heart is deceitful above all sir,
> Thus, spake Your servant, He ain't never said a truer word
> I find so many secrets locked inside of me
> And only You can make them known
> For only You possess the key and…

Our hearts can be broken in so many ways. Only God can lead us through the kind of detailed healing that we need. Throughout the years, I had come to realise that God wanted me to know the specifics of how He was healing me so that my awareness of the possibilities for how He heals others would expand. I had learned not to restrict what He wanted to do in my life or in the lives of others because of my limited understanding. I encouraged others to seek God for their healing and, in turn, be able to help those around them. There are no rules but many principles that can open our eyes to an awareness of the breadth and

---

75   Days of Elijah, Part of My Heart, Robin Mark, Novatech Studio, Belfast

depth of God's loving restoration in our lives. The form that His healing takes is personal and never repeated even within any subsequent healing of the same person. This throws us onto complete dependency on the Holy Spirit to help and guide us.

I now spent time reading my notes on what had been happening over the past two days. I wanted to see the big picture and grasp what God had been doing as He healed me, and so be sure that I had laid hold of it. I could now understand how antichrist spirits had been able to oppress me throughout my life by using fear and intimidation, and how this had interfered with my freedom. I felt such relief at the thought of being set free from such oppression. As I began to thank God and worship Him, I invited the Holy Spirit to fill me again. I sensed the words, "The Tartan Pimpernel,"[76] rising up from my spirit. This autobiographical book is about Donald Caskie, minister of the Scots Kirk in Paris, at the time of the German invasion of France in 1940, and how he helped to establish a network of safe houses and escape routes for allied soldiers and airmen trapped in occupied territory. He showed resourcefulness and courage in aiding thousands to freedom through his selfless commitment to others. I asked, "Why are you pointing to this?" "Forecast" was the reply. "You have provided and will provide a safe place for those escaping from the enemy."

I had come to the end of my three days of spiritual fast, but I was enjoying the time and space with God so much that I wanted to continue on my journey with God as much as I could whilst allowing for the responsibilities I had. Over the following few weeks, I continued to receive further healing of my heart and changing of faulty mindsets. A couple of months later, I awoke with the words rising from my spirit,

"I was made to worship. I was made to bless Your Name."[77]

---

76 The Tartan Pimpernel, Donald Caskie, 1957
77 Endless Praise, Made for Worship, Planetshakers, 2015

and then

"As a deer pants for water so my soul longs for you...."[78]

There then followed several insights from scripture; the woman at the well (John 4: 1-39), living water flowing from within (John 7: 37-38), water flowing from under the Temple (Ezekiel 47). I felt immersed in and consumed by God.

I thought about the gifts of God and how they are always good. I continued worshipping Him with thanksgiving for what He had given me and entrusted to me. He reminded me that I had been given the tongue of a ready writer[79] and would be able to flow His words to others. Psalm 87:3 came to mind,

"Glorious things are said of you, O City of God........of Zion it will be said, 'This one and that one were born in her, and the Most High will establish her."

The glorious things spoken of Zion by the Spirit are all pointing to Christ. While praying one morning two days later words rose up from my spirit,

"I am seated in the heavenly places in Christ."[80]

followed by,

"The effective prayer of a righteous man."[81]

A few days after this, as I woke up, I heard the word, "knock" so clearly. I've always been cautious so I asked what was behind the door I was to knock on!

---

78 "As the Deer", Martin J Nystrom, 1984
79 Psalm 45:1, 2
80 Ephesians 2: 6 paraphrased
81 James 5:16b paraphrased

I heard the words,

> "Divine health. Divine love."

Further words flowed,

> *"Keep on asking and you will receive what you ask for."* Matthew 7:7a

For a couple of years, I had been asking for a baptism of fire and, for some thirty years, for healing of my back,

> *"Keep on seeking and you will find."* Matthew 7: 7b

For a long, long time, I had been seeking to be free from fear and to know the love of God for me.

> *"Keep on knocking and the door will be opened to you."* Matthew 7:7c

This was what I had just been invited to do and, having responded, I had received divine health and divine love. This passage in Matthew instructs us,

> *"For everyone who asks receives. Everyone who seeks finds. And to everyone who knocks the door will be opened... ...So if you sinful people know how to give good gifts to your children, how much more will your heavenly Father give good gifts to those who ask Him."* Matthew 7: 8,11

Music and lyrics from a song rose up in my spirit,

> "You are the God that healeth me
> You are the Lord, my Healer
> You sent Your word and You healed my disease
> You are the Lord, my Healer."[82]

---

82 Worship with Don Moen, I am the God that Healeth Thee, 1993

As I got out of bed, I realised that my back had been healed. After thirty years of praying and waiting, the time had finally arrived. How excited I was! Over twenty-five years previously God had given me a promise that my back would be healed when I stopped allowing people to walk over it (Isaiah 51:23). It had taken all that time to be fully released from the root causes that had led to the back problems. Throughout this time, I had learnt so much from Him and about Him but, far more life changing, was that I had come to know Him as my Father who loves me and walks with me through every difficulty and triumph. He is my friend as well as being the One whom I worship and adore. All praise be to His glorious Name!

Some days later, I was thanking God that I was positioned in Christ Jesus in the heavenly realms and that I had been gifted with "divine health" and "divine love". I sensed His life pulsating through me and, as I read Matthew 8:22 that morning, it was as if Jesus said to me loud and clear,

"Follow Me now."

The emphasis was on the word, "now" and I sensed that following Him would be different now in some way. I knew with deep conviction that these words had taken on new meaning and life for me, and that I was entering onto new paths in divine love. I was full of anticipation. The next day was my birthday - a day of celebration!

Although my story continues, I have chosen to finish at this point. The three days of fasting on scripture while secluded with my Father God had turned my world upside down. No longer do I have overwhelming fear when confronted. Where before I would have been frozen with terror and unable to speak, now, when confronted, I can think and respond sensibly. Previously I could not feel the love of God within me but now I am bathed in His beautiful, amazing love all the time. Where before I found security in being needed, I now have total security and value just in belonging to my heavenly Father. Not only can I stand for long periods of time without back pain but I can stand emotionally strong against fear and spiritually strong against antichrist spirits.

I am deeply thankful to Father, Son and Spirit: to my Father God for His unconditional, faithful love; to my Saviour and Lord, Jesus Christ, through whom this transformation has been made possible; and to the gentle Holy Spirit who has shone His light on my path, leading me step by step. May you also enjoy spending unhurried time with our heavenly Father, communing with Him and entering into greater freedom in spirit, soul and body.

> Some birds live in cages[83]
> They never learn to fly
> And like those birds,
> I never found my wings
> But Lord, your love released me
> So I could see the sky
> And now my heart rejoices as I sing
>
> Spirit Wings,
> You lift me over all
> the earth-bound things
> And like a bird,
> my heart is flying free
> I'm soaring on the song
> your spirit brings
> O Lord of all,
> You let me see
> A vision of,
> your majesty
> You lift me up

---

83 Spirit Wings, Joni Eareckson, Album Spirit Wings, 2014

And carry me on your spirit wings

Now when I'm feeling lonely
I just look at You
And soon my heart is soaring high above
Everything is clearer
From Your point of view
Lifted up on spirit wings of love

Spirit Wings,
You lift me over all
the earth-bound things
And like a bird,
my heart is flying free
I'm soaring on the song
your spirit brings
O Lord of all,
You let me see
A vision of,
your majesty
You lift me up

And carry me on your spirit wings…

SECTION 6

OUR FATHER'S LOVE SONG OVER US

"The Lord your God is in your midst, a mighty one who will save; he will rejoice over you with gladness; he will quiet you by his love; he will exult over you with loud singing."

Zephaniah 3:17 ESV

Chapter 6.1
Our Father God's Love For us

> *"If you ask me why I love him so, O brides-to-be, it's because there is none like him to me. Everything about him fills me with holy desire! And now he is my beloved—my friend forever."*
> Song of Songs 5:16 TPT

One morning, several months after my three-day spiritual fast, I awoke in response to a gentle voice wooing me with the words, *"Come into the Holy of Holies"* and then sensed them retreating deep within me. I was caught up in the wonder that God would think of some part deep within me as the Holy of Holies and yet it made sense because I know that He dwells within me through His Holy Spirit. I lay pondering the wonder of this revelation, almost afraid to move and lose the moment. The truth gradually began to fill my whole being with sheer wonder and joy. Now, being fully aware of the presence of my Father God within me, that was drawing me into reverence and worship but also into exuberant anticipation and joyfulness in this affirming revelation of who I am, truly a new creation in Christ. Through this revelation, God was reminding me that I am the temple of the Holy Spirit,

> *"Have you forgotten that your body is now the sacred temple of the Spirit of Holiness, who lives in you? You don't belong to yourself any longer, for the gift of God, the Holy Spirit, lives inside your sanctuary."*
> 1 Corinthians 6:19 TPT

I had been feeling drawn towards reading Song of Songs in the Passion Translation again and as I began to read, was reminded of the truths within which had taken me on my journey with God out of fear and into divine love.

In this remarkable book in scripture there are some kernels of truth which apply to all spiritual and emotional healing through the Holy Spirit. For this reason, I want to share some insights from this translation as a conclusion to the many ministry insights shared throughout these books.[84]

Slowly pondering each verse, I came to chapter two and began reading,

> *"Let me describe him: he is graceful as a gazelle, swift as a wild stag. Now he comes closer, even to the places where I hide. He gazes into my soul, peering through the portal as he blossoms within my heart."*
> Song of Songs 2:9 TPT

The Shepherd comes close, seeing into our souls and the places where we hide. Little by little He helps us to come out of hiding, receive forgiveness and be healed so that we become progressively free. Through release, we are enabled to yield more and more to Him, and our hearts blossom increasingly with His presence (in the garden in our hearts). He has greater freedom within us and through us to minister His love to us and to others.

Over the years I have met many who love God with all their heart and who serve Him well but who have very little if any, awareness within of being deeply loved by God as their heavenly Father. Despite this, they live by faith in God and in His love for them. This kind of faith where we believe without seeing is commended by Jesus,

> *"Thomas, now that you've seen me, you believe. But there are those who have never seen me with their eyes but have believed*

---

[84] *The Ministry of the Father's Heart*, Books 1-3

in me with their hearts, and they will be blessed even more!"
John 20:29 TPT

Our desire to be closer to God beckons us as we journey through healings that dismantle our blockages step by step. Brian Simmons, in his translation, writes this,

"Who is this one? Look at her now! She arises out of her desert, clinging to her beloved. When I awakened you under the apple tree, as you were feasting upon me, I awakened your innermost being with the travail of birth as you longed for more of me." Song of Songs 8:5 TPT

You will recall that, in the previous chapter in which I described my journey out of fear and into divine love, I experienced, *"the travail of birth"* as God re-birthed part of my heart. My journey had, like that of the Shulammite bride, begun with longing in my heart for closer intimacy with God. In response to our longing, He welcomes us,

"Arise, my dearest. Hurry, my darling. Come away with me! I have come as you have asked to draw you to my heart and lead you out. For now, is the time, my beautiful one." Song of Songs 2:10 TPT

As we grow in awareness at heart level that we are totally and unreservedly loved by God, we become secure, no longer doubting like a wave of the sea[85] but deepening our faith in Him. We become unshakeable and fearless.

Later, as the Shulammite bride responds to the Bridegroom-King, He says to her,

"Can you not discern this new day of destiny breaking forth around you? The early signs of my purposes and plans are bursting forth. The budding vines of new life are now blooming everywhere. The fragrance of their flowers whispers, 'There is change in the air.' Arise,

---

85 James 1:6

my love, my beautiful companion, and run with me to the higher place. For now, is the time to arise and come away with me." Song of Songs 2:13 TPT

As I write, I am at present in ministry with someone who has suffered so much trauma in early childhood that it led to her having fragmented child-parts and alter egos. The effect on her as an adult has been devastating, to the extent that she has been barely able to communicate with others because of fear. As God has restored each child-part, releasing them from the rejection, misperceptions and lies that they have lived with, I have witnessed a step-by-step growth in confidence and in her ability to believe that she can achieve what had seemed impossible. She is enjoying the security of her heavenly Father's love and the freedom from fear. Each healing is drawing her closer and closer to the plans and purposes God has for her.

Earlier in Song of Songs we read,

"I am truly his rose, the very theme of his song. I'm overshadowed by his love, growing in the valley!" Song of Songs 2:1 TPT

In the hard times when we feel as though we are in a valley, we are still overshadowed by His love. We are truly His rose, flowering ever more beautifully. It is good to remember this when we are going through a see-saw of emotional healing from past hurts, are bewildered by the strangeness of emotions caused by having fragmented parts or a broken heart, or are struggling with what seems to be an uncontrollable bout of anger or inexplicable panic and fear. Always, our Father God overshadows us with His love, singing over us,

"For the Lord your God is living among you. He is a mighty Saviour. He will take delight in you with gladness. With his love, he will calm all your fears. He will rejoice over you with joyful songs." Zephaniah 3: 17 NLT

Deep healing takes time and cannot be rushed. We simply keep step with the One who heals. He invites us to,

> *"catch the troubling foxes, those sly little foxes that hinder our relationship. For they raid our budding vineyard of love to ruin what I've planted within you. Will you catch them and remove them for me? We will do it together."* Song of Songs 2:15 TPT

As God works with us to remove the "little foxes", He encourages us to keep trusting Him. We are invited by our Bridegroom-King to enter in through the archway of trust,

> *"Now you are ready, my bride, to come with me as we climb the highest peaks together. Come with me through the archway of trust. We will look down from the crest of the glistening mounts and from the summit of our sublime sanctuary. Together we will wage war in the lion's den and the leopard's lair as they watch nightly for their prey."* Song of Songs 4:8 TPT

He says to the Shulammite bride and to us,

> *"We will enhance your beauty, encircling you with our golden reins of love. You will be marked with our redeeming grace."* Song of Songs 1:11 TPT

words that clearly indicate that each person in the Godhead is fully devoted to nurturing us into the likeness of Jesus. How wonderful to know that we are in the centre of a circle of love formed by Father, Son and Holy Spirit speaking and acting together in unity for our good.

We can pray using these words from the Shulammite bride,

> *"Awake, O north wind!*
>
> *Awake, O south wind!*

Breathe on my garden with your Spirit-Wind.

Stir up the sweet spice of your life within me. Spare nothing as you make me your fruitful garden. Hold nothing back until I release your fragrance. Come walk with me as you walked with Adam in your paradise garden. Come taste the fruits of your life in me." Song of Songs 4:16 TPT

Brian Simmons explains[86],

> The Hebrew word for "north" comes from the root word for "hidden", "to treasure up" or "hidden (ones)". It takes both the cold north wind (God's hidden ways) and the south wind (God's pleasant, refreshing dealings with us) to bring forth the fragrance of His life in us and to saturate us with divine aromas.

> The scene of the garden and the breath of God point us back to Eden. Now this paradise is found in the bride (of Christ). This is the reason the reference to Adam is given: to help the reader connect with the mystery of the scene. See Jeremiah 31:12; John 15:1, 2.

The garden of our heart is where He works with us to remove the briers, thorns and weeds so that He can plant beautiful fruit and flowers, creating within us His paradise garden, a garden in which He enjoys spending time with us.

As we emerge from our cocoons of hiddenness and separation to soar in freedom with our Bridegroom-King these words resonate with us,

> *"Who is this one? She arises out of her desert, clinging to her beloved. When I awakened you under the apple tree, as you were feasting upon me, I awakened your innermost being with the travail of birth as you longed for more of me. Fasten me upon your heart as a seal of fire forevermore. This living, consuming flame will seal you as my*

---

86 Song of Songs 4:16a (footnote). The Passion Translation

prisoner of love. My passion is stronger than the chains of death and the grave, all-consuming as the very flashes of fire from the burning heart of God. Place this fierce, unrelenting fire over your entire being. Rivers of pain and persecution will never extinguish this flame. Endless floods will be unable to quench this raging fire that burns within you. Everything will be consumed. It will stop at nothing as you yield everything to this furious fire until it won't even seem to you like a sacrifice anymore." Song of Songs 8:5-7

Glossary

spirit: the part of us that is given a new nature, aligned with the Spirit of God, after we have invited Jesus into our lives. Our spirit can have a dynamic relationship with God.

soul: mind, emotions and will which is not given a new nature when we invite Jesus into our lives, but begins a life of transformation under the leading of the Holy Spirit, bringing us into alignment with our new nature.

intermingled: interwoven

healing: the process of making or becoming sound or healthy again *(https://dictionary.cambridge.org › dictionary)*

Contact The Author

office@MinistryoftheFathersHeart.com

Visit our website to learn more

www.MinistryoftheFathersHeart.com

Inspired To Write A Book?

Contact

Maurice Wylie Media

Your Inspirational & Christian Publisher

Based in Northern Ireland and distributing around the world.

www.MauriceWylieMedia.com

www.ingramcontent.com/pod-product-compliance
Lightning Source LLC
Chambersburg PA
CBHW041316110526
44591CB00021B/2801